NOT WITHOUT BLOOD

BLOOD

Understanding the New Covenant

2nd Edition

For My Parents
Louis and Evelyn Goldstein

ISBN: 13: 978-0692263778
ISBN: 10: 0692263772

Not Without Blood
Sheila R. Vitale

Living Epistles Ministries
Sheila R. Vitale
P O Box 562
Port Jefferson Station, NY 11776-0562 USA
(631) 331-1493

Living Epistles Ministries

Sheila R. Vitale
Pastor, Teacher, Founder
PO Box 562
Port Jefferson Station, NY 11776 USA

NOT WITHOUT BLOOD
Understanding The New Covenant
2nd Edition

Edited and Adapted as a Book by
Sheila R. Vitale

NOT WITHOUT BLOOD
Understanding The New Covenant

Is an adaptation of a Transcript of LEM Message
#304, Not Without Blood
Transcribed and Edited For
Clarity, Continuity of Thought, and Punctuation by
The LEM Transcribing and Editing Team

Formatted as a Book by
The LEM Professional Software Specialist Staff

Living Epistles Ministries
~ Judeo-Christian Spiritual Philosophy ~
Sheila R. Vitale
Pastor, Teacher & Founder

Ministry Staff
Anthony Milton, Teacher (South Carolina)
Brooke Paige, Teacher (New York)
Sandra Aldrich (MN) (July 7, 1975 – April 18, 2021)

Administrative Staff
Susan Panebianco, Office Manager

Editorial Staff
Rose Herczeg, Editor

Technical Staff
Lape Mobolaji-Lawal, Database Administrator

Ministry Illustrators
Cecilia H. Bryant (Oct. 18, 1921 – Oct. 23, 2013)
Fidelis Onwubueke

Music Staff
June Eble, Singer, Lyricist and Clarinetist
(July 20, 1931 – Jan. 24, 2024)
Don Gervais, Singer, Lyricist and Guitarist
Rita L. Rora, Singer, Lyricist and Guitarist

Table of Contents

The Alternate Translation Bible©

The Alternate Translation Bible (ATB)
Is an original interpretation of the Scripture.
It is not intended to replace traditional translations.

Alternate Translation of the Old Testament©
Alternate Translation, Exodus, Chapter 32
   (Crime of the Calf)©
Alternate Translation, Daniel, Chapter 8©
Alternate Translation, Daniel, Chapter 11©
Alternate Translation, Genesis 9:18-27
   (The Noah Chronicles, Second Edition) ©

Alternate Translation of the New Testament©
Alternate Translation, 2 Thessalonians, Chapter 2
   (Sophia)©
Alternate Translation, 1st John, Chapter 5©
Alternate Translation, the Book of Colossians
   (To The Church At Colosse)©
Alternate Translation, the Book of Ephesians
   (To The Church At Ephesus)©
Alternate Translation, the Book of Corinthians, Chapter 11
   (Corinthian Confusion)©
Alternate Translation, the Book of Jude
   (The Common Salvation)©

Alternate Translation of the Book of the Revelation of
   Jesus Christ to St. John©
Traducción Alternada del Libro de Revelación de Jesucristo©

ALTERNATE TRANSLATIONS IN THIS BOOK

NOT WITHOUT BLOOD

BLOOD

Understanding the New Covenant

2nd Edition

PROPHECY

Yea, saith the Lord, it is the hour for righteousness to appear in the earth. I shall stand once again, saith the Lord, in the fullness of my life, and I shall be exalted, and I shall be glorified in my people, and they shall judge the earth, saith the Lord.

They shall ascend unto Mt. Zion, and from there shall go forth the law, and from Jerusalem the Word, saith your God. And I shall be exalted, and every knee shall bow and every tongue confess and shall show my greatness, saith the Lord, and I shall bring into submission the most wicked of men saith God, even the workers of witchcraft.

I warn you, saith the Lord, against Pharisaical attitudes. Any one of my sons who criticizes me is in danger of losing their salvation. Put your eyes upon yourselves and do not blaspheme against who you will see coming into the Kingdom in these next days, saith the Lord, for you will be surprised at who I will bring in from the highways and the byways.

Exalt not yourself saith the Lord, knowing that you are not [fully] saved and that you are in as great a danger as anyone else of being separated from me.

Humble yourself and confess your sins and forgive one another, saith the Lord, and reconcile; be merciful to one another and fight the good fight of faith, for I will permit great hostility to come against you in these last days, saith the Lord, for this is the way that you will ascend. As you overcome, you shall ascend, and the stronger you get, the stronger the resistance I shall send against you.

War shall rage everywhere saith the Lord. There shall be wars and rumors of wars, and you shall war in your sleep and there shall be bloodshed and grief on every side saith the Lord, but my Son and the great dragon and his angels shall fight, saith the Lord, and Michael shall fight, and my sons, and they shall prevail over the dragon, saith the Lord, and I shall stand upon the earth, and my mercy shall be manifested to humanity.

INTRODUCTION

Jesus & the Paschal Lamb

The New Covenant is in the spiritual Blood of the Lord Jesus Christ.

The Blood of the Lord Jesus is in Christ Jesus, his Son.

The New Covenant is Eternal Life, in the flesh.

Eternal Life in the flesh is Christ Jesus resurrected in the individual.

Christ Jesus is the paschal lamb.

Ex 12:3 – *A Lamb for A Family*

> [3] SPEAK YE UNTO ALL THE CONGREGATION OF ISRAEL, SAYING, IN THE TENTH DAY OF THIS MONTH THEY SHALL TAKE TO THEM EVERY MAN A LAMB, ACCORDING TO THE HOUSE OF THEIR FATHERS, A LAMB FOR AN HOUSE: **KJV**

Understanding the Word of God fulfills the commandment to eat the paschal lamb, and understanding with the Mind of Christ, our higher mind, fulfills the commandment to put the blood of the paschal lamb on the doorpost.

Ex 12:7 – *Blood On The Carnal Mind*

> [7] AND THEY SHALL TAKE OF THE BLOOD, AND STRIKE IT ON THE TWO SIDE POSTS AND ON THE UPPER DOOR POST OF THE HOUSES, WHEREIN THEY SHALL EAT IT. **KJV**

In The Beginning

Gen 3:6 – *Forbidden Fruit*

> ⁶ AND WHEN THE WOMAN SAW THAT THE TREE WAS
> GOOD FOR FOOD, AND THAT IT WAS PLEASANT TO THE EYES,
> AND A TREE TO BE DESIRED TO MAKE ONE WISE, **SHE TOOK
> OF THE FRUIT THEREOF,** AND DID EAT, AND GAVE ALSO
> UNTO HER HUSBAND WITH HER; AND HE DID EAT. **KJV**

One single act of spiritual adultery . . .

Gen 3:6 – *Sin In The Garden*

> ⁶ AND WHEN THE WOMAN SAW THAT THE TREE WAS
> GOOD FOR FOOD, AND THAT IT WAS PLEASANT TO THE EYES,
> AND A TREE TO BE DESIRED TO MAKE ONE WISE, SHE TOOK OF
> THE FRUIT THEREOF, **AND DID EAT, AND GAVE ALSO UNTO
> HER HUSBAND WITH HER; AND HE DID EAT. KJV**

resulted in the death of Adam . . .

Gen 2:21 – *Sleep of Death*

> ²¹ **AND THE LORD GOD CAUSED A DEEP SLEEP TO
> FALL UPON ADAM** AND HE SLEPT: AND HE TOOK ONE OF HIS
> RIBS, AND CLOSED UP THE FLESH INSTEAD THEREOF; **KJV**

the exile of Cain . . .

Gen 4:14 – *Cain Banished*

> ¹⁴ BEHOLD, **THOU HAST DRIVEN ME OUT THIS DAY
> FROM THE FACE OF THE EARTH;** AND FROM THY FACE
> SHALL I BE HID; AND I SHALL BE A FUGITIVE AND A
> VAGABOND IN THE EARTH; AND IT SHALL COME TO PASS,
> THAT EVERY ONE THAT FINDETH ME SHALL SLAY ME. **KJV**

and the sale of Adam's descendants to Satan . . .

Rom 7:14 – *Sold Under Sin*

> [14] FOR WE KNOW THAT THE LAW IS SPIRITUAL: BUT I AM CARNAL, **SOLD UNDER SIN**. **KJV**

until the promised Redemption.

Eph 1:7, 14 – *Redemption through His Blood*

> [7] IN WHOM WE HAVE **REDEMPTION THROUGH HIS BLOOD, THE FORGIVENESS OF SINS,** ACCORDING TO THE RICHES OF HIS GRACE;

> [14] WHICH IS **THE EARNEST [DOWN PAYMENT] OF OUR INHERITANCE** UNTIL THE REDEMPTION OF THE PURCHASED POSSESSION, UNTO THE PRAISE OF HIS GLORY. **KJV**

Blood for Blood

Ex 21:23 – *Jehovah's vengeance*

> [23] AND IF ANY MISCHIEF FOLLOW, THEN THOU SHALT GIVE **LIFE FOR LIFE**, **KJV**

Abel was Jehovah's high priest in Paradise until his brother, Cain, slew him. After that, Cain tried to assume the office of high priest, . . .

Gen 4:4 – *Abel Preferred*

> [4] AND ABEL, HE ALSO BROUGHT OF THE FIRSTLINGS OF HIS FLOCK AND OF THE FAT THEREOF. AND **THE LORD HAD RESPECT UNTO ABEL AND TO HIS OFFERING**: KJV

but Jehovah banished him from the Garden.

Gen 4:14 – *Cain Banished*

> [14] BEHOLD, **THOU HAST DRIVEN ME OUT THIS DAY FROM THE FACE OF THE EARTH;** AND FROM THY FACE SHALL I BE HID; AND I SHALL BE A FUGITIVE AND A VAGABOND IN THE EARTH; AND IT SHALL COME TO PASS, THAT EVERY ONE THAT FINDETH ME SHALL SLAY ME. **KJV**

In addition to the judgment that fell on Cain, the child born of the adultery between the woman and the Serpent, . . .

Gen 3:16 – *Desire For Her Husband*

> [16] UNTO THE WOMAN HE SAID, I WILL GREATLY MULTIPLY THY SORROW AND THY CONCEPTION; **IN SORROW THOU SHALT BRING FORTH CHILDREN;** AND **THY DESIRE SHALL BE TO THY HUSBAND,** AND HE SHALL RULE OVER THEE. **KJV**

Jehovah turned the Woman over to the Serpent to experience the consequences of her choice.

Cain is the conscious part of the Mind of the Old Man of fallen mankind, and . . .

Col 3:9 – *Old Man*

> [9] LIE NOT ONE TO ANOTHER, SEEING THAT **YE HAVE PUT OFF THE OLD MAN WITH HIS DEEDS; KJV**

Christ Jesus, the regenerated Adam, is the New Man.

Eph 4:24 – *New Man*

> [24] AND THAT YE **PUT ON THE NEW MAN,** WHICH AFTER GOD IS CREATED IN RIGHTEOUSNESS AND TRUE HOLINESS. **KJV**

Jesus is the shape of the Father, and . . .

<u>John 14:9</u> – *Jesus' Father*

> ⁹ JESUS SAITH UNTO HIM, HAVE I BEEN SO LONG TIME WITH YOU, AND YET HAST THOU NOT KNOWN ME, PHILIP? **HE THAT HATH SEEN ME HATH SEEN THE FATHER;** AND HOW SAYEST THOU THEN, SHEW US THE FATHER? **KJV**

Cain is in the shape of the Serpent.

<u>2 Thess 2:9</u> – *Cain's Father*

> ⁹ EVEN HIM, **WHOSE COMING IS AFTER THE WORKING OF SATAN** WITH ALL POWER AND SIGNS AND LYING WONDERS, **KJV**

Cain is the First Born fruit of the Woman's adultery with the Serpent.

Satan, the enforcer of Jehovah's righteous Sowing & Reaping Judgment, was dispatched to kill Cain immediately after the murder of Abel . . .

<u>Job 1:6</u> – *Satan, Jehovah's Enforcer*

> ⁶ NOW THERE WAS A DAY WHEN THE SONS OF GOD CAME TO PRESENT THEMSELVES BEFORE THE LORD, AND SATAN CAME ALSO AMONG THEM. **KJV**

but Jehovah preserved Cain's life . . .

<u>Gen 4:15</u> – *Mark of Cain*

> ¹⁵ AND THE LORD SAID UNTO HIM, THEREFORE WHOSOEVER SLAYETH CAIN, VENGEANCE SHALL BE TAKEN ON HIM SEVENFOLD. **AND THE LORD SET A MARK UPON CAIN, LEST ANY FINDING HIM SHOULD KILL HIM. KJV**

until the time of the redemption of the descendants of the First
Adam . . .

Eph 1:14 – *The Purchased Possession*

¹⁴ WHICH IS THE EARNEST OF OUR INHERITANCE
UNTIL THE REDEMPTION OF THE PURCHASED POSSESSION,
UNTO THE PRAISE OF HIS GLORY. **KJV**

1 Cor 15:45 – *The 1st Adam*

⁴⁵ AND SO IT IS WRITTEN, **THE FIRST MAN ADAM
WAS MADE A LIVING SOUL;** THE LAST ADAM WAS MADE A
QUICKENING SPIRIT. **KJV**

who, to this very day, are Satan's prisoners.

Ps 146:7 - *Prisoners*

⁷ WHICH EXECUTETH JUDGMENT FOR THE
OPPRESSED: WHICH GIVETH FOOD TO THE HUNGRY. **THE
LORD LOOSETH THE PRISONERS: KJV**

Coats of Skins

Thereafter, the Woman and her son, Cain, died to their
immortality, and in the days of Pe-leg . . .

Gen 10:25 – *Animal Bodies*

²⁵ AND UNTO EBER WERE BORN TWO SONS: THE
NAME OF ONE WAS PELEG; **FOR IN HIS DAYS WAS THE
EARTH DIVIDED;** AND HIS BROTHER'S NAME WAS JOKTAN.
KJV

the fifth generation after the flood, they were imprisoned within
many animal bodies and are now appearing together as the

unconscious and conscious parts of the Carnal Mind of Adam's descendants, the many members of mortal humanity.

Adam's Descendants

Mortal humanity are the descendants of Shem, Ham and Japheth, Jehovah's third attempt to restore the Woman to righteousness. But Shem, Ham and Japheth's righteous nature turned back to Cain, mankind's evil side

1 John 3:12 – *Mankind's Evil Side*

> [12] NOT AS **CAIN, WHO WAS OF THAT WICKED ONE,** AND SLEW HIS BROTHER. AND WHEREFORE SLEW HE HIM? BECAUSE **HIS OWN WORKS WERE EVIL,** AND HIS BROTHER'S RIGHTEOUS. **KJV**

Sheila R. Vitale

ISRAEL, JEHOVAH'S SOLUTION

Law vs Grace

Law

Israel was subjected to the Law of Ordinances . . .

Eph 2:15 - *Commandments*

> [15] HAVING ABOLISHED IN HIS FLESH THE ENMITY, EVEN **THE LAW OF COMMANDMENTS** CONTAINED IN ORDINANCES; FOR TO MAKE IN HIMSELF OF TWAIN ONE NEW MAN, SO MAKING PEACE; **KJV**

. . . which required animal sacrifices, because the righteous Mind of Christ was not yet available to put Cain and the whole Carnal Mind underfoot.

Today, many Jews continue to keep the Law in the hope that God will count that behavior for righteousness.

Rom 9:31-32 – *Righteousness by Faith*

> [31] **BUT ISRAEL, WHICH FOLLOWED AFTER THE LAW OF RIGHTEOUSNESS, HATH NOT ATTAINED TO THE LAW OF RIGHTEOUSNESS.**
>
> [32] WHEREFORE? BECAUSE THEY SOUGHT IT NOT BY FAITH, BUT AS IT WERE BY THE WORKS OF THE LAW. FOR THEY STUMBLED AT THAT STUMBLINGSTONE; **KJV**

Grace

Christ Jesus, man's glorious New Mind, consumes the animal nature every time sin is recognized and acknowledged, so it is no

1

longer necessary to kill the whole man, body and soul, because of sin, or to substitute animals for human flesh.

The Christians' hope for righteousness is in Jesus' Spiritual Blood painted on the side posts of their Carnal Mind.

Ex 12:23 – *Blood on the Side Posts*

> [23] FOR THE LORD WILL PASS THROUGH TO SMITE THE EGYPTIANS; AND WHEN HE SEETH **THE BLOOD UPON THE LINTEL, AND ON THE TWO SIDE POSTS,** THE LORD WILL PASS OVER THE DOOR, AND WILL NOT SUFFER THE DESTROYER TO COME IN UNTO YOUR HOUSES TO SMITE YOU. **KJV**

A Relationship with God

In the days of Queen Esther, anyone who came into the king's presence, even the queen, would die if the king did not hold out his scepter to them.

Est 4:11 - *Golden Sceptre*

> [11] ALL THE KING'S SERVANTS, AND THE PEOPLE OF THE KING'S PROVINCES, DO KNOW, THAT WHOSOEVER, WHETHER MAN OR WOMAN, SHALL COME UNTO THE KING INTO THE INNER COURT, WHO IS NOT CALLED, THERE IS ONE LAW OF HIS TO PUT HIM TO DEATH, EXCEPT SUCH TO WHOM **THE KING SHALL HOLD OUT THE GOLDEN SCEPTRE, THAT HE MAY LIVE:** BUT I HAVE NOT BEEN CALLED TO COME IN UNTO THE KING THESE THIRTY DAYS. **KJV**

Why would coming near to God result in death?

Mankind is filled with sin, and when sin comes in contact with the holiness of God, sin, and the vessel that contains it, both die.

Ex 20:19 – *Hearing God Speak*

> [19] AND THEY SAID UNTO MOSES, SPEAK THOU WITH US, AND WE WILL HEAR: BUT **LET NOT GOD SPEAK WITH US, LEST WE DIE.** KJV

But, today, through the spiritual Blood of Jesus Christ, the whole world has the opportunity to enter into God's presence with impunity.

Jehovah has given the world a special dispensation through the Lord Jesus Christ.

Jehovah made a covenant with us, saying, *obey me, love the Lord your God with all your heart, your mind and your soul; love your brother as yourself . . .*

Matt 22:37-40 – *Love The Lord*

> [37] JESUS SAID UNTO HIM, THOU SHALT LOVE THE LORD THY GOD WITH ALL THY HEART, AND WITH ALL THY SOUL, AND WITH ALL THY MIND.
>
> [38] THIS IS THE FIRST AND GREAT COMMANDMENT.
>
> [39] AND THE SECOND IS LIKE UNTO IT, THOU SHALT LOVE THY NEIGHBOUR AS THYSELF.
>
> [40] **ON THESE TWO COMMANDMENTS HANG ALL THE LAW AND THE PROPHETS.** KJV

. . . cease from fornication, blood and things strangled . . .

Acts 15:29 – *Abstain From Unclean Things*

> [29] THAT YE **ABSTAIN FROM MEATS OFFERED TO IDOLS, AND FROM BLOOD, AND FROM THINGS STRANGLED, AND FROM FORNICATION:** FROM WHICH IF YE KEEP YOURSELVES, YE SHALL DO WELL. FARE YE WELL. **KJV**

. . . and Christ Jesus will cover your sins.

James 5:20 – *Sins Covered*

> [20] LET HIM KNOW, THAT **HE WHICH CONVERTETH THE SINNER** FROM THE ERROR OF HIS WAY SHALL SAVE A SOUL FROM DEATH, AND SHALL HIDE A MULTITUDE OF SINS. **KJV**

We can walk with him, and talk with him, and receive the blessings of healing and deliverance in this world.

The Pursuit of Immortality

But no one, as yet, neither Jew nor Christian, has laid hold of the promise of the Scripture, which is *Everlasting Life*, even immortality in the flesh, without torment.

Prov 10:22 – *Blessings without Sorrow*

> [22] THE BLESSING OF THE LORD, IT MAKETH RICH, AND HE ADDETH **NO SORROW** WITH IT. **KJV**

What the Church calls *the New Testament* is a record of Jesus of Nazareth, the first man to experience True Immortality, and the unfolding of the Scriptures which prophesy Jehovah's previously sealed up *Plan of Redemption.*

1 Tim 6:16 - *Immortality*

> [16] **WHO ONLY HATH IMMORTALITY,** DWELLING IN THE LIGHT WHICH NO MAN CAN APPROACH UNTO; WHOM NO MAN HATH SEEN, NOR CAN SEE: TO WHOM BE HONOUR AND POWER EVERLASTING. AMEN. **KJV**

Jehovah offered Israel Immortality, Everlasting Life, with the first set of tablets that Moses brought down from Mt. Sinai.

After those tablets were broken . . .

Ex 32:19 – *1ˢᵗ Set of Tablets Broken*

> ¹⁹ AND IT CAME TO PASS, AS SOON AS HE CAME NIGH UNTO THE CAMP, THAT HE SAW THE CALF, AND THE DANCING: AND MOSES' ANGER WAXED HOT, AND **HE CAST THE TABLES OUT OF HIS HANDS, AND BRAKE THEM BENEATH THE MOUNT. KJV**

. .. Jehovah forgave Israel for making a golden calf . . .

Ex 32:24 – *Golden Calf*

> ²⁴ AND I SAID UNTO THEM, WHOSOEVER HATH ANY GOLD, LET THEM BREAK IT OFF. SO THEY GAVE IT ME: THEN I CAST IT INTO THE FIRE, AND **THERE CAME OUT THIS CALF. KJV**

. . . and granted them a relationship with Himself through Moses, His appointed Mediator.

1 Tim 2:5 – *One Mediator*

> ⁵ FOR THERE IS ONE GOD, AND **ONE MEDIATOR BETWEEN GOD AND MEN**, THE MAN CHRIST JESUS; **KJV**

Today, Immortality, Everlasting Life, is found only in the New Covenant, which is in the spiritual Blood of the glorified Jesus Christ.

Wherefore, Christ Jesus is now the only Mediator between God and Man.

TWO COVENANTS
IN THE CHURCH

The Jew believes that he will return to Adam's first estate, and higher, by performing good works.

The Christian believes that he will be raptured away from the problems of this present world, to live in a mansion located in a place called *Heaven*.

The truth, though, is that all mankind, Jew and Christian alike, have been offered amnesty in the form of *the forgiveness of sins*.

Matt 13:52 – *The Old & The New*

> [52] THEN SAID HE UNTO THEM, THEREFORE EVERY SCRIBE WHICH IS INSTRUCTED UNTO THE KINGDOM OF HEAVEN IS LIKE UNTO A MAN THAT IS AN HOUSEHOLDER, **WHICH BRINGETH FORTH OUT OF HIS TREASURE THINGS NEW AND OLD. KJV**

We are taught that the Church is under the New Covenant, but it has been obvious for a long time that there must be something wrong with this teaching.

Why?

Because Christians continue to get sick and die just like the rest of humanity, and the promise of *Everlasting Life*, Immortality in the flesh, the foundational principle of the New Covenant, is not manifesting in the Church.

Rom 6:22 – *Everlasting Life*

> [22] BUT NOW BEING MADE FREE FROM SIN, AND BECOME SERVANTS TO GOD, YE HAVE YOUR FRUIT UNTO HOLINESS, AND THE **END EVERLASTING LIFE. KJV**

Why?

Because the Church has not been taught what the part of the individual believer is, in the process that leads to the promised Immortality in the flesh.

Why?

Because the Carnal Mind of fallen humanity, which partakes of the New Covenant by faith, cannot understand *Jehovah's Plan of Redemption*. Only the Christ Mind can understand it.

So, in the absence of the Truth, the Church embraces Egyptian Mystery Religion, which teaches that we go to a place called *Heaven* after our physical body dies.

THE OLD COVENANT
IN THE CHURCH

Jehovah's Covenant with National Israel went to the Gentiles because the Jews stumbled.

> **Rom 9:32** – *The stumbling stone*
>
> [32] WHEREFORE? BECAUSE THEY SOUGHT IT NOT BY FAITH, BUT AS IT WERE BY THE WORKS OF THE LAW. FOR **THEY STUMBLED AT THAT STUMBLING STONE; KJV**

The same Old Covenant which was given to the Jew first, went to the Greek also, but in a different form.

The spoken Word that falls on one lady, affects her one way, and when it falls on another lady, affects her another way.

The same Word of God helped both ladies, but not in the same way. The same Word mixed with each individual mind and spirit to produce a personalized spiritual experience for each lady.

The Old Covenant falls one way on the Jew, and a second way on the Greek (Gentile), but it's still *the Old Covenant*.

How do I know that the Old Covenant, as well as *the beginning phases* of the New Covenant are operating in the Church today?

Because everlasting life is nowhere to be seen.

The Sowing & Reaping Judgment

The Old Covenant provides a way to escape death, the ultimate result of sin, through obedience to the Law of Ordinances

9

Col 2:14 – *The Law of Ordinances*

¹⁴ BLOTTING OUT ***THE HANDWRITING OF ORDINANCES*** THAT WAS AGAINST US, WHICH WAS CONTRARY TO US, AND TOOK IT OUT OF THE WAY, NAILING IT TO HIS CROSS; **KJV**

Jehovah's righteous Sowing & Reaping Judgment enforces the Old Covenant . . .

Gal 6:7 – *Sowing & Reaping*

⁷ BE NOT DECEIVED; GOD IS NOT MOCKED: FOR **WHATSOEVER A MAN SOWETH, THAT SHALL HE ALSO REAP. KJV**

. . . which is unto destruction.

Obedience to the Law of Ordinances satisfied the Sowing & Reaping Judgment for National Israel, and

Obedience to *Jehovah's Moral Laws*, as taught by Jesus, satisfies the Sowing & Reaping Judgment for spiritual Israel.

Matt 22:37-40 – *Love the Lord*

³⁷ JESUS SAID UNTO HIM, **THOU SHALT LOVE THE LORD THY GOD WITH ALL THY HEART, AND WITH ALL THY SOUL, AND WITH ALL THY MIND.**

³⁸ THIS IS THE FIRST AND GREAT COMMANDMENT.

³⁹ AND THE SECOND IS LIKE UNTO IT, **THOU SHALT LOVE THY NEIGHBOUR AS THYSELF.**

⁴⁰ ON THESE TWO COMMANDMENTS HANG ALL THE LAW AND THE PROPHETS. **KJV**

<u>Matt 19:18-19</u> – *Love Your Neighbor*

[18] HE SAITH UNTO HIM, WHICH? JESUS SAID, **THOU SHALT DO NO MURDER,** THOU SHALT NOT COMMIT **ADULTERY,** THOU SHALT NOT STEAL, THOU SHALT NOT **BEAR FALSE WITNESS,**

[19] **HONOUR THY FATHER AND THY MOTHER:** AND, THOU SHALT LOVE THY NEIGHBOUR AS THYSELF. **KJV**

THE NEW COVENANT

The Substitution of Souls

The physical flesh of the men who marry Christ Jesus and overcome their sin nature does not die.

Their Carnal Mind dies.

The seed of Jesus Christ, the regenerated male Adam . . .

Matt 19:28 - *Regeneration*

> [28] AND JESUS SAID UNTO THEM, VERILY I SAY UNTO YOU, THAT YE WHICH HAVE FOLLOWED ME, **IN THE REGENERATION WHEN THE SON OF MAN SHALL SIT IN THE THRONE OF HIS GLORY,** YE ALSO SHALL SIT UPON TWELVE THRONES, JUDGING THE TWELVE TRIBES OF ISRAEL. **KJV**

. . . awakens Abel, the root of the dead female Adam within all men . . .

Job 14:8-9 – *Alive Again*

> [8] THOUGH THE ROOT THEREOF WAX OLD IN THE EARTH, AND THE STOCK THEREOF DIE IN THE GROUND;
>
> [9] YET THROUGH THE SCENT OF WATER **IT WILL BUD, AND BRING FORTH BOUGHS LIKE A PLANT. KJV**

. . . and the two Adams mature into the spiritual man, Christ Jesus, who is destined to marry the Lord Jesus Christ, the Saviour of the personality.

1 Thess 4:17 – *Forever With The Lord*

> [17] THEN WE WHICH ARE ALIVE AND REMAIN SHALL BE CAUGHT UP TOGETHER WITH THEM IN THE CLOUDS, TO

MEET THE LORD IN THE AIR: AND SO SHALL WE EVER BE WITH
THE LORD. **KJV**

After that, Christ Jesus swallows up the fallen nature of mortal
mankind, the physical body is preserved, and everlasting life is
imparted to the whole man, right here in this present world.

This is the truth of the ***substitutionary work*** of the glorified Jesus
Christ: The resurrected life of Christ Jesus, internalized within a
personality, overshadows and eventually nullifies the deadly
influence of the Carnal Mind.

We are saved from judgment by living in the Spirit . . .

1 Peter 4:6 – *Judged In The Flesh*

[6] FOR, FOR THIS CAUSE WAS THE GOSPEL PREACHED
ALSO TO THEM THAT ARE DEAD, THAT THEY MIGHT BE
JUDGED ACCORDING TO MEN IN THE FLESH, BUT LIVE
ACCORDING TO GOD IN THE SPIRIT. **KJV**

. . . and that whoever walks after the Spirit, is called a Son of
God.

Rom 8:14 – *Sons of God*

[14] FOR AS MANY AS ARE **LED BY THE SPIRIT** OF
GOD, THEY ARE THE SONS OF GOD. **KJV**

The Lord Jesus Christ is calling us to be a spiritual people, to
have the Spirit that raised Christ from the dead dwell in us,
prevail over our Carnal Mind and quicken our mortal body/[1]
BEFORE our physical body is in the grave.

---

[1] Mortal soul, or personality.

<u>1 Cor 15:55</u> – *Death Defeated*

[55] O DEATH, WHERE IS THY STING? O GRAVE, WHERE IS THY VICTORY? **KJV**

TWO SPIRITS IN THE CHURCH

The Spirit of Christ and *the Holy Spirit* are two different administrations of the Spirit of God.

1 Cor 12:5 – *Two Spirits, One Source*

> ⁵ AND THERE ARE **DIFFERENCES OF ADMINISTRATIONS**, BUT THE SAME LORD. **KJV**

The Holy Spirit

The Holy Spirit is female.

The Holy Spirit is called *grace*, *unmerited favor*, because it carries the virile *female* seed of the Lord Jesus Christ, which is the beginning of the promised *Regeneration of Righteousness*.

Matt 19:28 - *Regeneration*

> ²⁸ AND JESUS SAID UNTO THEM, VERILY I SAY UNTO YOU, THAT YE WHICH HAVE FOLLOWED ME, **IN THE REGENERATION WHEN THE SON OF MAN SHALL SIT IN THE THRONE OF HIS GLORY,** YE ALSO SHALL SIT UPON TWELVE THRONES, JUDGING THE TWELVE TRIBES OF ISRAEL. **KJV**

The Holy Spirit is *Jehovah's mercy* to mankind.

The Holy Spirit of Jesus Christ carries Jesus' female seed.

Jesus' female seed saves the human spirit.[2]

---

[2]   See, the discussion about how the female seed of the Lord Jesus Christ is awakening Abel, Adam's dead female seed of the previous age, in *Christ vs the Christ Consciousness*, below.

A Free Gift

Jehovah gave **the Holy Spirit** to fallen mankind as a **free gift**, because there is nothing that mankind can do to restore itself to eternal life.

Rom 5:15 – *Gift of Grace*

> [15] BUT NOT AS THE OFFENCE, SO ALSO IS THE FREE GIFT. FOR IF THROUGH THE OFFENCE OF ONE MANY BE DEAD, MUCH MORE THE GRACE OF GOD, AND **THE GIFT BY GRACE,** WHICH IS BY ONE MAN, JESUS CHRIST, HATH ABOUNDED UNTO MANY. **KJV**

Rom 5:15 - AT: *If the sin of one man, Adam, can result in the many members of mankind dying, then,* **the gift of God, which is the grace that is given to humanity through one man, Jesus Christ,** *should be able to affect the many members of mankind also* **ATB**

Rom 5:16 - *No Condemnation*

> [16] AND NOT AS IT WAS BY ONE THAT SINNED, SO IS THE GIFT: FOR THE JUDGMENT WAS **BY ONE TO CONDEMNATION,** BUT THE FREE GIFT IS **OF MANY OFFENCES UNTO JUSTIFICATION. KJV**

Rom 5:16 - AT: *But [the effect of the one who brought] the free gift is not the same as [the effect of] the one who sinned, because [Jehovah's] legal judgment condemned one man, but the free gift justifies many sinners,* **ATB**

Rom 5:17 – *Gift of Righteousness*

> [17] FOR IF BY ONE MAN'S OFFENCE DEATH REIGNED BY ONE; MUCH MORE THEY WHICH RECEIVE ABUNDANCE OF GRACE AND OF **THE GIFT OF RIGHTEOUSNESS SHALL REIGN IN LIFE BY ONE, JESUS CHRIST. KJV**

Rom 5:17 - AT: *So, if the sin committed by one man caused death to reign [over all of mankind], then, how much more shall an abundance of righteousness reign in the lives of those who receive the gift of grace through Jesus Christ* **ATB**

<u>Rom 5:18</u> – *Justification unto Life*

[18] THEREFORE AS BY THE OFFENCE OF ONE JUDGMENT CAME UPON ALL MEN TO CONDEMNATION; EVEN SO BY **THE RIGHTEOUSNESS OF ONE THE FREE GIFT CAME UPON ALL MEN UNTO JUSTIFICATION OF LIFE. KJV**

Rom 5:18 - AT: *Therefore, since the sin of one man resulted in the judgment that condemned all men [to death], then [I conclude, says Paul], that the free gift [must have restored] all men to life through Jesus Christ, the one righteous [man, who] justified [their sins]* **ATB**

The Holy Spirit influences us towards righteousness.

<u>Rom 14:17</u> – *Spiritual Blessings*

[17] FOR **THE KINGDOM OF GOD** IS NOT MEAT AND DRINK; BUT RIGHTEOUSNESS, AND PEACE, AND JOY IN THE HOLY GHOST. **KJV**

Rom 14:17 - AT: *The righteousness, peace and joy of the Kingdom of God is in the Holy Spirit, not in the spiritual philosophy*3 *[of this world]* **ATB**.

The Spirit of Christ

The Spirit of Christ is male.

The Spirit of Christ is the Spirit in the man, Christ Jesus.

---

[3]   Translation of ***meat and drink***

19

Rom 8:11 – *Jesus, The Man; Christ, The seed*

[11] BUT IF THE SPIRIT OF HIM **THAT RAISED UP JESUS FROM THE DEAD** DWELL IN YOU, **HE THAT RAISED UP CHRIST FROM THE DEAD** SHALL ALSO QUICKEN YOUR MORTAL BODIES BY HIS SPIRIT THAT DWELLETH IN YOU. **KJV**

If the Spirit that raised Jesus of Nazareth from the dead in his glorified body dwells in you, that same Spirit will awaken the dead Christ from the previous age within you, and the resurrected Christ will give life to your personality (mortal body, or soul).[4]

The Spirit of Christ operates in tandem with the Mind of Christ, which is being formed in the sons of God.

1 Cor 2:16 – *The Mind of Christ*

[16] FOR WHO HATH KNOWN THE MIND OF THE LORD, THAT HE MAY INSTRUCT HIM? BUT WE HAVE **THE MIND OF CHRIST. KJV**

The Spirit of Christ, that dwells with Christ . . .

Prov 8:12 – *Wisdom & Knowledge*

[12] I WISDOM DWELL WITH PRUDENCE, AND FIND OUT KNOWLEDGE OF WITTY INVENTIONS. **KJV**

. . . preserves the personality (mortal soul), and ushers her into the age abiding, endless life of the Lord Jesus Christ, right here in this present world.

---

[4]   See, *Hope of Glorification*, above, and *Christ vs Christ Consciousness*, below, for an explanation of the resurrection of Christ in the individual.

TWO CHRISTS

Christ

Christ, the Lad

Christ is a translation of the Greek word that means *the anointing*.

In the New Testament, the word, *Christ*, has multiple meanings.

The Christ, is Jesus in the days of his flesh.

Christ, is the virile seed of the glorified Jesus Christ.

Christ is sometimes referred to as a *lad*, or *a young man*.

Christ is the nature of God.

2 Cor 4:4 – *The Image of God*

> [4] IN WHOM THE GOD OF THIS WORLD HATH BLINDED THE MINDS OF THEM WHICH BELIEVE NOT, LEST THE LIGHT OF THE GLORIOUS GOSPEL OF **CHRIST, WHO IS THE IMAGE OF GOD**, SHOULD SHINE UNTO THEM. **KJV**

Christ is the beginning of Christ Jesus, Jesus' spiritual manhood within humanity.

Col 1:27 - *Hope of Glorification*

> [27] TO WHOM GOD WOULD MAKE KNOWN WHAT IS THE RICHES OF THE GLORY OF THIS MYSTERY AMONG THE GENTILES; WHICH IS **CHRIST IN YOU, THE HOPE OF GLORY**: **KJV**

Christ, the Man

Christ, the *male* seed of the Lord Jesus Christ, joins with Jesus' *female* seed to produce *Christ Jesus*, the savior of the personality.

The man, Christ Jesus, saves the personality (soul) of the man that he is born in.

Christ Jesus is the full-grown spiritual man in a human being. The destiny of *Christ Jesus* is to marry the Lord Jesus Christ and be the permanent link between God and the man that he is attached to.

2 Tim 1:10 – *Christ Jesus, Savior*

> [10] AND WHICH NOW HAS BEEN MANIFESTED THROUGH THE APPEARING OF **OUR SAVIOR CHRIST JESUS,** WHO ABOLISHED DEATH AND BROUGHT LIFE AND IMMORTALITY TO LIGHT THROUGH THE GOSPEL, **ESV**

Christ Jesus, joined to the Lord Jesus Christ, is called *the Lamb of God.*

The Lamb of God is the savior of the physical body that Christ Jesus is born in, through the forgiveness of sin.

John 1:29 – *Lamb of God*

> [29] THE NEXT DAY JOHN SEETH JESUS COMING UNTO HIM, AND SAITH, BEHOLD **THE LAMB OF GOD, WHICH TAKETH AWAY THE SIN OF THE WORLD. KJV**

The Christ Consciousness

Mortal humanity are the descendants of the First Adam who died to his immortality when the Woman agreed with the thoughts of the Serpent.

Christ, in this context, is the dead, female seed of the First Adam, who, today, is a part of the mortal foundation of all human beings. We call this dead Christ, *Abel*, who was slain by his brother, Cain, to distinguish him from *the living Christ seed* that the Lord Jesus Christ is sowing into the Israel of God today.

It is taught by some that *Abel*, the dead, female seed of a previous age, is the living **Christ Consciousness,** the innate intelligence that is within all men from birth.

On the contrary, *Abel*, the Christ that we are born with, is bound to the *sin consciousness* that was birthed through the Woman's adultery with the Serpent, and is, therefore, born dead.

Rom 8:10 – *Born Dead*

> [10] AND IF CHRIST BE IN YOU, **THE BODY IS DEAD BECAUSE OF SIN**; BUT THE SPIRIT IS LIFE BECAUSE OF RIGHTEOUSNESS. **KJV**

Mortal humanity is born dead and *unaware* of God because of the First Adam's sin. Indeed, this dead Christ is the spiritual source of *the sleeping beauty myth*.

Abel is sleeping the sleep of death in most mortal men, and the Spirit of Jesus Christ is the only way for him to be resurrected.

1 Cor 15:22 – *Life Through Christ*

> [22] FOR AS IN ADAM ALL DIE, EVEN SO **IN CHRIST SHALL ALL BE MADE ALIVE**. **KJV**

The dead Christ within mortal humanity will awaken . . .

1 Cor 15:34 - *Righteousness*

> [34] **AWAKE TO RIGHTEOUSNESS**, AND SIN NOT; FOR SOME HAVE NOT THE KNOWLEDGE OF GOD: I SPEAK THIS TO YOUR SHAME. **KJV**

. . . to ***the God consciousness*** that the First Adam lost, when the Lord Jesus Christ, the Son of God, kisses him.

Ps 2:12 – *Spiritual Kisses*

> [12] KISS THE SON, LEST HE BE ANGRY, AND YE PERISH FROM THE WAY, WHEN HIS WRATH IS KINDLED BUT A LITTLE. BLESSED ARE ALL THEY THAT PUT THEIR TRUST IN HIM. **KJV**

The word ***kiss*** is a metaphor for the spiritual union between the Lord Jesus Christ and ***Abel***, ***the dead Christ*** within a mortal man.

1 Cor 6:17 – *One Spirit*

> [17] BUT HE THAT IS **JOINED UNTO THE LORD IS ONE SPIRIT**. **KJV**

The male seed of the glorified Jesus Christ must join with Abel, the dead, female seed of the First Adam, mankind's mortal foundation, for Christ Jesus, mankind's ***regenerated*** . . .

Matt 19:28 - *Regeneration*

> [28] AND JESUS SAID UNTO THEM, VERILY I SAY UNTO YOU, THAT YE WHICH HAVE FOLLOWED ME, **IN THE REGENERATION** WHEN THE SON OF MAN SHALL SIT IN THE THRONE OF HIS GLORY, YE ALSO SHALL SIT UPON TWELVE THRONES, JUDGING THE TWELVE TRIBES OF ISRAEL. **KJV**

. . . God consciousness . . .

1 Cor 1:30 – *Wisdom, etc.*

> [30] BUT OF HIM ARE YE IN CHRIST JESUS, WHO OF GOD IS MADE UNTO US **WISDOM**, AND **RIGHTEOUSNESS**, AND **SANCTIFICATION**, AND **REDEMPTION**: **KJV**

. . . to be born again.

1 Peter 1:23 – *Born Again*

[23] BEING BORN AGAIN, NOT OF CORRUPTIBLE SEED, BUT OF INCORRUPTIBLE, BY THE WORD OF GOD, WHICH LIVETH AND ABIDETH FOR EVER. **KJV**

IMMORTALITY

Jesus Could Have Lived Forever

No one could take the life of Jesus, the Christ, in the days of his flesh without his permission. Jesus could have lived in the flesh forever, but, rather, chose, of his own free will, to lay down his perfected earthly life, to ascend to a high spiritual place from where he became Saviour of the physical bodies . . .

Eph 5:23 – *Saviour of The Body*

> [23] FOR THE HUSBAND IS THE HEAD OF THE WIFE, EVEN AS CHRIST IS THE HEAD OF THE CHURCH: AND HE IS THE **SAVIOUR OF THE BODY. KJV**

of mankind.

A Season for Immortality

Paul set forth this same truth, that no one could take his life without his permission.

2 Tim 4:6 – *Paul Offered*

> [6] FOR **I AM NOW READY TO BE OFFERED**, AND THE TIME OF MY DEPARTURE IS AT HAND. **KJV**

Paul said that it was time for him *to be offered*, thereby implying *ascension*, rather than *death*. Paul would have lived forever, in the flesh, if he had ascended in the spiritual season that supports eternal life in this world.

But, Paul was born out of season . . .

2 Tim 4:2 – *Spiritual Seasons*

> [2] Preach the word; **be instant in season, out of season**; reprove, rebuke, exhort with all longsuffering and doctrine. **KJV**

. . . meaning that it was not yet time for Jesus' spiritual offspring to live in the flesh forever, in this world.

Paul stayed around long enough to write a large part of the New Testament, and then gave up an existence which had the potential to continue forever.

Christ Jesus was born within Paul before the spiritual season in which humanity will be permitted to return to immortality, so Paul was taken from this world.

The significance of the word, *offered*, is that Paul was qualified to have his physical body adopted. Paul did not die because of sin. He was taken from this world because the spiritual mechanism that converts the physical body, was not yet operational.

Brethren, the season for men to begin the process that transforms the bestial mind that we are born with into the spiritual Mind of the Lord Jesus Christ which enables us to live forever, has begun!

The New Covenant, brethren, is Everlasting Life B Immortality in the flesh!

Brethren, if your walk with Jesus Christ has not produced Everlasting Life, if you are still getting sick, and aging -- if you are still dying, you have not yet fully entered into the New Covenant!

If this truth is upsetting you, rebuke your distress, because you have nothing to worry about if it is a lie!

On the other hand, if I am telling you the truth, Jesus said that the truth will set you free

28

John 8:32 – *Truth Is Liberating*

> [32] AND YE SHALL KNOW THE TRUTH, AND **THE TRUTH SHALL MAKE YOU FREE. KJV**

We are saved by a spiritual union with the Son of God, brethren. We are not saved by doctrine. Lies cannot destroy our relationship with Jesus Christ. He will deliver us from every error that we become embroiled in, if we are truly joined to him.

Whoever is joined to the Spirit of the Son, receives Everlasting Life.

1 Cor 6:17 –*Joined To The Lord*

> [17] BUT HE THAT IS JOINED UNTO **THE LORD IS ONE SPIRIT. KJV**

There must be something wrong with the teaching in the Church, brethren, because many believers are still getting sick and experiencing defeat at the hands of Satan. Something must be wrong with the doctrine, because people are still dying!

The Church is lacking the information that we need to enter into life, and this is the information:

THREE PHASES OF
THE NEW COVENANT

There are three phases of the New Covenant:

Redemption of the Spirit[5]

The human spirit is redeemed when it is pierced by the Holy Spirit of Jesus Christ.

Gal 2:20 – *Live By The Faith*

> [20] I AM CRUCIFIED WITH CHRIST: NEVERTHELESS I LIVE; YET NOT I, BUT CHRIST LIVETH IN ME: AND THE LIFE WHICH I NOW LIVE IN THE FLESH I LIVE **BY THE FAITH OF THE SON OF GOD**, WHO LOVED ME, AND GAVE HIMSELF FOR ME. **KJV**

Rev 1:7 – *Behold He Cometh*

> [7] BEHOLD, HE COMETH WITH CLOUDS; AND EVERY EYE SHALL SEE HIM, AND THEY ALSO WHICH PIERCED HIM: AND ALL KINDREDS OF THE EARTH SHALL WAIL BECAUSE OF HIM. EVEN SO, AMEN. **KJV**

Rev 1:7 – AT: *Look! He is coming in [many] spiritual bodies, and every[one whose human spirit is] pierced by him, shall see him, and the [many] races [who inhabit] the earth shall certainly be cut down because of [his spiritual Blood], amen. ATB*

The spiritual Blood of Jesus Christ is creating a new, single nation, and bringing into existence the true and *Righteous One World Order.*

---

[5] See, *The Common Salvation* (by Sheila R. Vitale, published by Living Epistles Ministries, Create Space 2014)

Acts 17:26 – *One Blood*

> [26] AND HATH **MADE OF ONE BLOOD ALL NATIONS OF ME**N FOR TO DWELL ON ALL THE FACE OF THE EARTH, AND HATH DETERMINED THE TIMES BEFORE APPOINTED, AND THE BOUNDS OF THEIR HABITATION; **KJV**

Salvation of the Soul (Personality)

Christ Jesus is the Mediator of the White Throne Judgment . . .

Rev 20:11 – *White Throne Judgment*

> [11] AND I SAW **A GREAT WHITE THRONE,** AND HIM THAT SAT ON IT, FROM WHOSE FACE THE EARTH AND THE HEAVEN FLED AWAY; AND THERE WAS FOUND NO PLACE FOR THEM. **KJV**

. . . which is corrective, works for our good, and leads to eternal life.

The forgiveness of sins by faith in Jesus Christ, saves the personality (soul) and delivers us from Satan's destruction in this present world.

We continue to sin and die during the first two phases of the New Covenant (Redemption of the human spirit and Salvation of the soul/personality), but *Christ Jesus is the merciful administrator of the consequences for all confessed sins*, and

Satan continues to enforce *the Sowing & Reaping Judgment*, which is unto destruction, *for all unconfessed sin. This is the Old Covenant that is still operating in the Church.*

The Adoption of the Physical Body

Two Kinds of Blood

The *mystery of the Gospel of Blood*, speaks about *two kinds of blood*, one holy and one unholy, the first polluting and the second purifying.

The Holy Blood

<u>Heb 9:11</u> – *Christ, High Priest*

> [11] BUT **CHRIST BEING COME AN HIGH PRIEST** OF GOOD THINGS TO COME, BY A GREATER AND MORE PERFECT TABERNACLE, NOT MADE WITH HANDS, THAT IS TO SAY, NOT OF THIS BUILDING; **KJV**

The Lord Jesus Christ is calling all of His people today, Jews and Gentiles alike, to enter into *the Heavenly Sanctuary* by the authority of His purifying Blood, which is the New Covenant.

<u>Heb 8:2</u> – *The Holy Place*

> [2] A MINISTER OF **THE SANCTUARY, AND OF THE TRUE TABERNACLE,** WHICH THE LORD PITCHED, AND NOT MAN. **KJV**

The blood that grants us *entrance* into the Heavenly Tabernacle is the glorified, *spiritual* Blood of the Lord Jesus Christ.

The Lord Jesus Christ is reproducing his resurrected life in mankind.

Christ Jesus is the Son of Jesus Christ.

Acts 4:30 – *Holy Child*

> [30] BY STRETCHING FORTH THINE HAND TO HEAL; AND THAT SIGNS AND WONDERS MAY BE DONE BY THE NAME OF **THY HOLY CHILD JESUS**. **KJV**

The Lord Jesus Christ is above, *Christ Jesus* is below.

Christ Jesus is Jesus' spiritual Blood in mankind.

Christ Jesus is mankind's inheritance.

Col 1:12 - *Inheritance*

> [12] GIVING THANKS UNTO THE FATHER, WHICH HATH MADE US MEET TO BE PARTAKERS OF **THE INHERITANCE OF THE SAINTS** IN LIGHT: **KJV**

Christ Jesus is mankind's New Inner Man.

Eph 3:16 – *Inner Man*

> [16] THAT HE WOULD GRANT YOU, ACCORDING TO THE RICHES OF HIS GLORY, TO BE STRENGTHENED WITH MIGHT BY HIS SPIRIT IN **THE INNER MAN**; **KJV**

Christ Jesus is the Everlasting Tabernacle.

The physical body of the man, *Jesus*, who was the Christ in the days of his flesh, was crucified, and his physical body was melted and then blended . . .

2 Peter 3:12 – *A Spiritual Body*

> [12] LOOKING FOR AND HASTING UNTO THE COMING OF THE DAY OF GOD, WHEREIN THE HEAVENS BEING ON FIRE SHALL BE DISSOLVED, AND **THE ELEMENTS SHALL MELT WITH FERVENT HEAT**? **KJV**

. . . with his spirit and sinless soul life, into a resurrected, spiritual man.

After that, Jesus ascended into a high spiritual place from where his resurrected life can now be grafted to fallen men.

The Blood Seed

The fruit of Jesus' sacrifice is *Christ*, the seed that produces *Christ Jesus, the Everlasting Tabernacle*, which is being formed within mankind.

Christ is the resurrected root of Adam of Creation, who died in his sins.

Christ Jesus, who is born from *Christ,* is *the Kingdom of God*.

The Kingdom of Heaven is the Kingdom of Darkness bound under the authority of *Christ Jesus, the Kingdom of God.*

Christ must be born again within us . . .

John 3:3 - *Born Again*

> [3] JESUS ANSWERED AND SAID UNTO HIM, VERILY, VERILY, I SAY UNTO THEE, **EXCEPT A MAN BE BORN AGAIN,** HE CANNOT SEE THE KINGDOM OF GOD. **KJV**

. . . if we are to see the Kingdom of God, because our human spirit, which is our God consciousness, cannot enter the Everlasting Tabernacle, or even see it, if that Tabernacle is not inside of us!

The Everlasting Tabernacle is accessible to us only when Christ Jesus is in the midst of us because *Christ Jesus IS the Everlasting Tabernacle.*

We enter into the Heavenly Tabernacle by Jesus' resurrected life, which is **Christ** grafted to our mortal foundation.

Christ Jesus is the only man who is strong enough to liberate the personalities of fallen mankind from the grip of Satan and Leviathan, the unconscious and subconscious parts of mankind's fallen mind.

Brethren, the blood that was in the body that Jesus was given, Jesus' human blood that bled onto the ground at Calvary, is not getting us into the Kingdom of Heaven.

It is **the spiritual Blood of Jesus' Father** that is saving us, and that resurrected Blood is Christ in you.

So, we have now learned that the spotless, spiritual Blood of the Lord Jesus Christ

(1)   Reconciles us to God and

(2)   Grants us access to the Everlasting Tabernacle, which is Eternal Life.

The Unholy Blood

The sacrifice for sins is a substitutionary work. This means that there are two elements to the process:

1. The part that is being replaced, and

2. The substitute part

Mankind's sin nature, our unholy spiritual blood, is being replaced with the holy spiritual Blood of a righteous nature, because only a righteous man can live forever.

FORGIVENESS FOR PAST SINS

The Old Covenant

Under the Old Covenant, the blood of bulls and goats rescinds, makes of no effect, the consequences to the soul, for sin.

How does the blood of bulls and goats blot out sin?

It does not.

In other words, forgiveness for sins under the Old Covenant means that the mandated *consequence to the soul* for sins, is not carried out. The potential to sin, the sin itself, or its influence, is not removed.

But sin rots the physical body and, thus, eventually the body and the personality (soul) die.

The New Covenant

There is forgiveness for sin under the New Covenant, but the individual believer must appropriate that forgiveness according to Jehovah's Rules and Regulations.

Acts 5:31 - *Forgiveness*

> [31] HIM HATH GOD EXALTED WITH HIS RIGHT HAND TO BE A PRINCE AND A SAVIOUR, FOR **TO GIVE REPENTANCE TO ISRAEL, AND FORGIVENESS OF SINS. KJV**

The New Covenant Is Superior

Reconciliation with God

The New Covenant is superior to the Old Covenant because, it offers *reconciliation with God*, . . .

2 Cor 5:20 – *Reconciliation With God*

[20] NOW THEN WE ARE AMBASSADORS FOR CHRIST,
AS THOUGH GOD DID BESEECH YOU BY US: WE PRAY YOU IN
CHRIST'S STEAD, **BE YE RECONCILED TO GOD. KJV**

Three Degrees of Forgiveness

The New Covenant provides for three degrees of forgiveness:

Forgiveness for **the human spiri**t,

Forgiveness for **the soul**, and

Forgiveness for Cain, **the animal body**

Christ, the spiritual Blood of Jesus in a man, is involved in all three processes of forgiveness.

Where *Christ* is invoked, as demonstrated by conviction of wrong-doing and remorse . . .

The consequence to the soul for sins IS RESCINDED,

But where *Christ is* **NOT** sincerely invoked,

The Sowing & Reaping Judgment, which is the Old Covenant judgment unto destruction,

. . . is still in full force and effect.

Non-Enforcement

Under both the Old and the New Covenants, where **there is no sorrow or conviction of sin,** the personality is under **the Sowing & Reaping Judgment unto destruction.**

So, we see that **the Levitical sacrifices for sins** under **the Old Covenant** and **the Redemption of The Human Spirit** & **the Salvation Of The Soul,** which are **the First Two Phases of the New Covenant,** are actually the **NON-ENFORCEMENT OF THE PENALTIES FOR SINS,** based upon certain prescribed behavior, rather than **the exchange** of one **Righteous Life** for many **sinful lives,**[6] which is **the reality of the New Covenant**

Rom 5:19 – *Many Made Righteous*

> [19] FOR AS BY ONE MAN'S DISOBEDIENCE MANY WERE MADE SINNERS, SO BY THE OBEDIENCE OF ONE SHALL MANY BE MADE RIGHTEOUS. **KJV**

Exchange of Souls

The New Covenant promise of a sacrifice for sins is fulfilled in the exchange of souls (personalities).

Exchange, in this context, means that we exchange our fallen soul for Jesus' sinless soul, called *Christ*.

Jesus' Blood for our blood.

This does not mean that Jesus gives up his righteous soul and takes on our fallen soul in its place. The exchange has to do with us alone. Jesus continues in his glorified state no matter what we do, and our sins cannot pollute him.

John 1:5 – *Incorruptible*

> [5] AND THE LIGHT SHINETH IN DARKNESS; AND **THE DARKNESS COMPREHENDED IT NOT. KJV**

The sacrifice for sins is our fallen soul. Our own blood.

---

[6]   See, *Blood for Blood* p 3

Under the Old Covenant, the blood of bulls and goats is substituted for our blood, the offering of which would kill us.

Under the first phase of the New Covenant, the spiritual Blood of Jesus covers our soul (personality).

Jehovah cannot see our sins, **so the penalty for sin is not enforced**.

Rom 11:29 – *No Penalty*

> [29] FOR THE GIFTS AND CALLING OF GOD ARE WITHOUT REPENTANCE. **KJV**

The exchange of our blood for the Blood of Jesus begins in the second phase of the New Covenant (Salvation of the soul) and is completed in the third phase (Adoption of the physical body).

Jesus' Blood

Jesus' *physical* blood does not blot out our sins.

Jesus' *spiritual* Blood blots out our sins, permanently, *when it replaces our human blood.*

Luke 24:39 – *Spiritual, Not Human Blood*

> [39] BEHOLD MY HANDS AND MY FEET, THAT IT IS I MYSELF: HANDLE ME, AND SEE; FOR A SPIRIT HATH NOT FLESH AND BONES, AS YE SEE ME HAVE. **KJV**

The body of the resurrected Jesus has flesh and bones. It does not have blood.

The words *blood* and *soul* (personality) are interchangeable.

Sinful Blood

The life of sinful flesh is in the blood, or in the soul.

For so long as any aspect of our fallen soul (personality) which is in the blood exists, we continue to be subject to death.

Wherefore, the blood that is *shed* for a sacrifice, is the blood of our own sin nature.

Death of the Sin Nature

We have an inheritance in heavenly places and that inheritance is Christ Jesus, but we must die to our sin nature to appropriate it.

The sin nature includes the emotions and the mind of the fallen soul (personality), called the *Carnal Mind*.

The mind is not in or a part of the physical brain. Mind is spiritual. It is distributed throughout the entire body, as is the blood, and even beyond the physical body.

The resurrection of Jesus, the Christ, made everlasting life available to all mankind, but to appropriate that life, for it to start manifesting itself in us, for it to become real to us, this new life which is in Christ Jesus must replace, must swallow up, our sin nature. Our Carnal Mind must die!

Rom 6:3 – *Baptized Into Death*

> [3] KNOW YE NOT, THAT SO MANY OF US AS WERE BAPTIZED INTO JESUS CHRIST WERE **BAPTIZED INTO HIS DEATH**? **KJV**

Our own Carnal Mind is the fulfillment of the bulls and goats that were sacrificed under the Old Covenant.

Our Carnal Mind is the Beast of Revelation that must be offered up for the promises which are in Christ Jesus to be implemented in our lives.

Yes, Jesus entered in by His sinless resurrected, spiritual blood, which is now poured out upon us as Christ, his male seed, our potential for the sinless Mind of Christ to be reproduced in us.

But when the Mind of Christ appears in us, we have two minds:

The *bestial Carnal Mind* that we are born with, and

The *glorious Mind of Christ* that we inherit.

Jesus & the Animal Sacrifice

The animal sacrifices of Leviticus do not typify Jesus' physical crucifixion.

They typify the sacrifice of our own bestial nature.

The fulfillment of the Levitical type of the blood of bulls and goats, *the blood which must be shed*, is not the blood of the Lord Jesus Christ, but the blood of our own bestial Carnal Mind, which pollutes us continually.

Now, if, in fact, the crucifixion of Jesus, the Christ, fulfilled the Old Testament type of the blood of bulls and goats, why was Jesus, the Christ, crucified, and not roasted?

Lev 1:13 – *Burnt Sacrifice*

[13] BUT HE SHALL WASH THE INWARDS AND THE LEGS WITH WATER: AND THE PRIEST SHALL BRING IT ALL, AND BURN IT UPON THE ALTAR: **IT IS A BURNT SACRIFICE,** AN OFFERING MADE BY FIRE, OF A SWEET SAVOUR UNTO THE LORD. **KJV**

Leviathan, The True Sacrifice

The method of Jesus' death does not line up with the way the bulls and goats were killed by the Hebrew priests.

I challenge all of you Pharisees who are still reading this book to explain why, if Jesus' crucifixion is the fulfillment of the Levitical animal sacrifices, Jesus, the Christ, was not roasted.

Christ Jesus, the Lake of Fire within a man, descends upon Satan and Leviathan, the unconscious and subconscious parts of that personality's Carnal Mind, to boil Satan and roast Leviathan.

Leviathan, the pride of man and the subconscious part of the Carnal Mind, is the true sacrifice that is roasted in the Lake of Fire.

This is the death of the Carnal Mind, the fallen soul (personality) of that man.

And when the fallen soul (personality) is consumed by Christ Jesus, Christ Jesus becomes the soul (personality) of the man that sacrificed it.

This is how we are saved from death and enter into the life of the ages, which is the fulfillment of the New Covenant.

ABRAHAM

Abraham's Spiritual Seed

The still unfulfilled promises that Jehovah made to Abraham are for Abraham's spiritual seed . . .

Gal 3:16 – *Christ, Abraham's seed . . .*

> ¹⁶ NOW TO **ABRAHAM** AND HIS SEED WERE THE PROMISES MADE. HE SAITH NOT, AND TO SEEDS, AS OF MANY; BUT AS OF ONE, AND TO THY **SEED, WHICH IS CHRIST**. **KJV**

. . . and Abraham's seed are the people who have inherited Abraham's nature, which is the nature of Christ.

Abraham's Physical Seed

The physical bodies of all nationalities and ethnicities, Jew and Gentile, alike, are clay containers for spiritual life.

Every physical body is formed from the nefesh grade of soul, which is the residue of fallen Adam.

Spiritually speaking, the only difference between the physical bodies of human beings, is that some physical bodies are inhabited by divinity, and others are not.

Rom 9:6 – *Not All Israel*

> ⁶ NOT AS THOUGH THE WORD OF GOD HATH TAKEN NONE EFFECT. FOR THEY ARE NOT ALL ISRAEL, WHICH ARE OF ISRAEL: **KJV**

Jesus said to the Pharisees, *I will tell you the truth and the truth will set you free,* and the Pharisees said, *what truth could you possibly have to tell us? . . .*

John 9:34 – *Pharisees Unteachable*

> [34] THEY ANSWERED AND SAID UNTO HIM, THOU WAST ALTOGETHER BORN IN SINS, AND **DOST THOU TEACH US**? AND THEY CAST HIM OUT. **KJV**

We are the seed of Abraham, and answer only to God.

John 8:33 – *Not bound to any man*

> [33] THEY ANSWERED HIM, WE BE ***ABRAHAM'S SEED***, AND **WERE NEVER IN BONDAGE TO ANY MAN**: HOW SAYEST THOU, YE SHALL BE MADE FREE? **KJV**

Salvation Not In the DNA

And Jesus answered, saying, this is the truth I have to tell you, all you Pharisees. You are not saved by your physical DNA.

You are carnal, fallen men. Dead men's bones.

Matt 23:27 – *Dead Men's Bones*

> [27] WOE UNTO YOU, SCRIBES AND PHARISEES, HYPOCRITES! FOR YE ARE LIKE UNTO WHITED SEPULCHRES, WHICH INDEED APPEAR BEAUTIFUL OUTWARD, BUT ARE WITHIN FULL OF **DEAD MEN'S BONES**, AND OF ALL UNCLEANNESS. **KJV**

You are spiritually dead because of your sins.

Col 2:13 – *Dead Because of Sin*

> [13] AND YOU, BEING **DEAD IN YOUR SINS** AND THE UNCIRCUMCISION OF YOUR FLESH, HATH HE QUICKENED TOGETHER WITH HIM, HAVING FORGIVEN YOU ALL TRESPASSES; **KJV**

Your behavior may have changed, but you are just as spiritually filthy as you were when you first started out.

Your righteousness is as filthy rags.

Isa 64:6 – *Filthy Rags*

> ⁶ BUT WE ARE ALL AS AN UNCLEAN THING, AND ALL *OUR RIGHTEOUSNESSES ARE AS FILTHY RAGS*; AND WE ALL DO FADE AS A LEAF; AND OUR INIQUITIES, LIKE THE WIND, HAVE TAKEN US AWAY. **KJV**

You need to recognize and confess the hidden sins of your heart, and repent, so that the Spirit of Christ can crucify (join with) your human spirit (the redemption of your spirit) . . .

Gal 2:20 – *Sin Nature Crucified*

> ²⁰ I AM **CRUCIFIED WITH CHRIST**: NEVERTHELESS I LIVE; YET NOT I, BUT CHRIST LIVETH IN ME: AND THE LIFE WHICH I NOW LIVE IN THE FLESH I LIVE BY THE FAITH OF THE SON OF GOD, WHO LOVED ME, AND GAVE HIMSELF FOR ME. **KJV**

. . . apply the Blood of the Lord Jesus Christ's everlasting sacrifice to your personality . . .

Ex 12:23 - *The Doorposts of Your Carnal Mind*

> ²³ FOR THE LORD WILL PASS THROUGH TO SMITE THE EGYPTIANS; AND **WHEN HE SEETH THE BLOOD** UPON THE LINTEL, AND **ON THE TWO SIDE POSTS**, THE LORD WILL PASS OVER THE DOOR, AND WILL NOT SUFFER THE DESTROYER TO COME IN UNTO YOUR HOUSES TO SMITE YOU. **KJV**

and translate you, the personality, into everlasting life.

And to all the Pharisees in the Church, Jesus is saying, your spirit is saved, but your soul (personality) is not saved yet, and **you are**

**still under the Old Covenant in every area where you are not
confessing your sins.**

You can scream and yell and deny it all that you like, but the hour
is at hand for the New Covenant to be implemented, and the
Father will take whoever He desires to take - with your consent,
or without your consent.

A NEW BLOODLINE

Acts 17:26 – *One New Bloodline*

²⁶ AND HATH MADE **OF ONE BLOOD ALL NATIONS** OF MEN FOR TO DWELL ON ALL THE FACE OF THE EARTH, AND HATH DETERMINED THE TIMES BEFORE APPOINTED, AND THE BOUNDS OF THEIR HABITATION; **KJV**

The Carnal Mind Must Die

We must die to our sin nature and live out of the Mind of Christ Jesus, the New Man that is being formed within us, if we are to overcome sin.

The unclean spirit of our Carnal Mind is the fallen, spiritual blood of mankind's dead sin nature

Mark 3:29-30 – *Satan, The Blaspheming Spirit*

²⁹ BUT HE THAT SHALL BLASPHEME AGAINST THE HOLY GHOST HATH NEVER **FORGIVENESS, BUT IS IN DANGER OF ETERNAL DAMNATION:**

³⁰ BECAUSE THEY SAID, HE HATH AN UNCLEAN SPIRIT. **KJV**

That dead spiritual blood must be shed if we are to enter into, Christ Jesus, the Tabernacle of Life which is within ourselves, and live out of Christ Jesus, our new spiritual bloodline.

Christ Raised

<u>Heb 9:13-14</u> – *Blood That Purges the Conscience*

> [13] FOR IF THE BLOOD OF BULLS AND OF GOATS, AND THE ASHES OF AN HEIFER SPRINKLING THE UNCLEAN, SANCTIFIETH TO **THE PURIFYING OF THE FLESH**:

> [14] HOW MUCH MORE SHALL THE BLOOD OF [THE] CHRIST[7] WHO THROUGH THE EVERLASTING SPIRIT OFFERED HIMSELF WITHOUT SPOT TO GOD, **PURGE YOUR CONSCIENCE FROM DEAD WORKS** TO SERVE THE LIVING GOD? **KJV**

Now follow me with this . . .

> *How much more shall the blood of the resurrected Christ who, through the everlasting Spirit . . .*

that is, the Spirit of Christ . . .

> *. . . offered himself without spot to God.*

This means that the spiritual blood of the resurrected Christ in the man, Jesus, purified Jesus' soul (personality) from sin.

Listen, let me show it to you again.

> *The blood of Jesus, the Christ, who through the everlasting Spirit . . .*

Not through the Holy Spirit, brethren, but through *the Spirit of Christ.*

---

[7]   According to the Greek, this is referring to the Lord Jesus Christ.

If that Spirit that raised Christ from the dead dwells in you, it will quicken, or make alive, *your mortal body*, that is, your soul (personality)

Rom 8:11 – *Christ Raised*

> [11] BUT IF THE SPIRIT OF HIM THAT RAISED UP JESUS FROM THE DEAD DWELL IN YOU, HE **THAT RAISED UP CHRIST FROM THE DEAD** SHALL ALSO QUICKEN YOUR MORTAL BODIES BY HIS SPIRIT THAT DWELLETH IN YOU. **KJV**

Your mortal body is your soul, or personality.

Why is your soul not being made alive like Jesus' soul was?

Because, the Scripture is talking about *the Spirit of Christ*, the Everlasting, Eternal Spirit, *not the Holy Spirit!*

Jesus Offers His Soul

The mystery of Jesus' sacrifice for sins is that he gave up his life in this world, but he did not die.

He gave up his existence in this world, and was rewarded with a higher form of existence.

So, we see that . . .

The blood of Christ . . .

within the man, Jesus . . .

> **who, through the Everlasting** [Eternal] **Spirit** [of the Father]**, offered himself** . . . .

Who is *himself,* brethren?

The resurrected Christ in the man, Jesus, offered up his own humanity (soul/personality) as a sacrifice to Jehovah, and Christ Jesus in you, is offering up your sin nature (Carnal Mind). Can you hear it? Listen, let's do it again.

How much more shall the blood of Christ. . .

. . . the resurrected spiritual life of Christ. . .

through the Everlasting Spirit, offer himself. . .

offer his humanity, or his soul, or his personality . . .

without spot. . . .

The resurrected Christ in the man, Jesus, purified Jesus, his humanity, his human side, from sin, and, then . . .

Jesus Offers His Body

Jesus, the purified soul man, the personality that was standing in front of Christ Jesus, offered his physical body to Jehovah.

1 Cor 15:28 – *Physical Body Offered*

> [28] AND WHEN ALL THINGS SHALL BE SUBDUED UNTO HIM, **THEN SHALL THE SON ALSO HIMSELF BE SUBJECT UNTO HIM THAT PUT ALL THINGS UNDER HIM**, THAT GOD MAY BE ALL IN ALL. **KJV**

The Potential to Sin

So, we see that Christ Jesus within us is exposing our sin nature, and purifying us from its deadly effects.

Now listen, brethren, you cannot be purified from the deadly effects of your sin nature, until your sin nature is exposed. We've discussed this over and over again, how *the true forgiveness of sins is the ripping out of the potential to sin*.

If the forgiveness of sins is merely the forgiveness of an act or a thought, then the confession of the Roman Catholic Church would be sufficient.

The Scripture clearly states that we have a sin nature and that we are spiritually dead because of that sin nature. So, if we are dead because of our *potential to sin*, which potential is resident in our sin nature, then *the true forgiveness of sins must be the wiping out, the obliteration, of our sin nature, which is our Carnal Mind*.

The man, Jesus, lived out of the resurrected Christ within himself, and overcame the potential to sin which was in the Carnal Mind that all men born of a flesh woman inherit.

So, we see that the indwelling Spirit of Christ purified the soul (personality) of the man, Jesus, and he became Jesus, the Christ.

Rom 1:4 – *Soul Purified*

4 AND DECLARED TO BE THE SON OF GOD WITH POWER, ACCORDING TO THE SPIRIT OF HOLINESS, BY THE RESURRECTION FROM THE DEAD: **KJV**

Jesus' Death & Resurrection

Luke 2:11 – *Birth of A Savior*

11 FOR UNTO YOU IS BORN THIS DAY IN THE CITY OF DAVID A SAVIOUR, WHICH IS CHRIST THE LORD. **KJV**

Jesus sacrificed his purified soul, and gave up his life as an immortal, spiritual man, to be translated into an even higher, spiritual form which could be grafted to the masses of fallen humanity.

Jesus was physically crucified only after Christ rose from the dead within him . . .

1 Cor 15:4 - *Christ Raised*

⁴ AND THAT HE WAS BURIED, AND THAT **HE ROSE AGAIN THE THIRD DAY ACCORDING TO THE SCRIPTURES:** **KJV**

. . . and crucified the Carnal Mind that was attached to the physical body that he, the man, Jesus received when he was born into this world.

Christ Jesus is the Savior of the body, but the immortal life that is in his spiritual Blood must be grafted to our soul for the power of his sacrifice to save us!

The Church has the same opportunity today that Jesus had to be purified from sin through the exposure and ripping out of our inherited sin nature.

He who hath this hope, brethren, that the dead Christ within him will be resurrected, purifies himself.

1 John 3:3 – *Reason For Hope*

³ AND **EVERY MAN THAT HATH THIS HOPE IN HIM PURIFIETH HIMSELF,** EVEN AS HE IS PURE. **KJV**

The White Throne Judgment

The Judgment Seat of Christ, which exposes the sin nature of the personality (soul) and brings it into submission to the Spirit of Holiness, is the only path to true purification.

Christ Jesus within us forces our sin nature (Carnal Mind) under his spiritual feet . . .

Mal 4:3 – *Sin Nature Forced Under*

³ AND YE SHALL TREAD DOWN THE WICKED; FOR **THEY SHALL BE ASHES UNDER THE SOLES OF YOUR FEET** IN

THE DAY THAT I SHALL DO THIS, SAITH THE LORD OF HOSTS.
KJV

. . . and our Carnal Mind is renewed or reformed . . .

Eph 4:23 – *Spiritual Renewal*

²³ AND **BE RENEWED IN THE SPIRIT OF YOUR MIND;**
KJV

. . . in the image of Christ. After that, he offers our spotless soul (personality) to the Everlasting Spirit. . . if you can hear it.

A Purified Conscience

How much more will Jesus' spiritual Blood, which now is in the form of the Spirit of Christ, purge our conscience from dead works?

Heb 9:14 – *Spiritual Blood*

¹⁴ **HOW MUCH MORE SHALL THE BLOOD OF THE CHRIST, WHO THROUGH THE EVERLASTING SPIRIT OFFERED HIMSELF WITHOUT SPOT TO GOD** PURGE YOUR CONSCIENCE FROM DEAD WORKS TO SERVE THE LIVING GOD? **KJV**

The question is, if the blood of bulls and goats can sanctify and purify your flesh, how much more will the Blood of Christ Jesus sanctify and purify your conscience?

The Greek word translated *conscience* means *mind*. We are talking about *the purification of the mind*.

The Old Covenant deals with the sins of the flesh and teaches Israel to resist behavioral and verbal sin.

The New Covenant deals with the potential for sin that is in the mind. Christ Jesus renews the spirit of our Carnal Mind and reforms it into the Mind of Christ, an incorruptible mind, which is *incapable of sin*.

Eph 4:23 – *Mind Renewed*

²³ AND BE RENEWED IN THE SPIRIT OF YOUR MIND;
KJV

Purged From Sin

How does the resurrected spiritual Blood of Jesus, the Christ, purge us from our potential for sin?

The resurrected, spiritual Blood of the Lord Jesus Christ is given to us, initially, as the Holy Spirit, the female seed of Christ Jesus. After that, it is given as the male seed called **Christ**, which is grafted to Abel, the male side of our mortal foundation.

We, the personality (soul), then join with Christ in the effort to purify ourselves by exposing our sin nature, and then paralyzing and eventually destroying the *potential for sin* within ourselves.

Can you hear it? Let me say it again.

The Lord Jesus Christ purges our conscience, our mind, from sin, by grafting his glorified life (spiritual Blood) to the male side of our mortal foundation.

Christ Jesus is, then, born from that foundation within us, to judge our sin-filled personality (soul), which judgment saves us from our own Carnal Mind's potential to sin.

Obad 21 – *Saviors From Zion*

²¹ AND SAVIOURS SHALL COME UP ON MOUNT ZION TO JUDGE THE MOUNT OF ESAU; AND THE KINGDOM SHALL BE THE LORD'S. **KJV**

In the hour that Christ Jesus brings our personality (soul) into complete submission to *the Spirit of Holiness which is in Christ Jesus* (who began to be formed in us when Christ was grafted to our mortal foundation), he separates our personality (soul) from our sin nature, and offers up our spotless personality (soul) to the Father.

How does Christ Jesus purify our personality (soul) to the point that she will be without sin?

There's only one way brethren, by burning our Old Man in the Lake of Fire (Christ Jesus) . . .

Rev 20:10 - *Lake of Fire*

> [10] AND THE DEVIL THAT DECEIVED THEM WAS CAST INTO THE **LAKE OF FIRE AND BRIMSTONE,** WHERE THE BEAST AND THE FALSE PROPHET ARE, AND SHALL BE TORMENTED DAY AND NIGHT FOR EVER AND EVER. **KJV**

. . . where our personality (soul) is divided from our Carnal Mind, . . .

Heb 4:12 –*Soul Divided*

> [12] FOR THE WORD OF GOD IS QUICK, AND POWERFUL, AND SHARPER THAN ANY TWOEDGED SWORD, PIERCING EVEN TO **THE DIVIDING ASUNDER OF SOUL AND SPIRIT, AND OF THE JOINTS AND MARROW,** AND IS A DISCERNER OF THE THOUGHTS AND INTENTS OF THE HEART. **KJV**

. . . which is ripped to pieces, as the elements of our sin nature melt and come crashing down.

Dan 3:25 – *Surviving the Fire*

²⁵ HE ANSWERED AND SAID, LO, I SEE FOUR MEN LOOSE, **WALKING IN THE MIDST OF THE FIRE, AND THEY HAVE NO HURT**; AND THE FORM OF THE FOURTH IS LIKE THE SON OF GOD. **KJV**

2 Peter 3:10,12 – *Heavens Melted*

¹⁰ BUT THE DAY OF THE LORD WILL COME AS A THIEF IN THE NIGHT; IN THE WHICH **THE HEAVENS SHALL PASS AWAY WITH A GREAT NOISE,** AND **THE ELEMENTS SHALL MELT WITH FERVENT HEAT,** THE EARTH ALSO AND THE WORKS THAT ARE THEREIN SHALL BE BURNED UP.

¹² LOOKING FOR AND HASTING UNTO THE COMING OF THE DAY OF GOD, WHEREIN **THE HEAVENS BEING ON FIRE** SHALL BE DISSOLVED, AND **THE ELEMENTS SHALL MELT WITH FERVENT HEAT**? **KJV**

Then we, the personality (soul), marry and become one with Christ Jesus, the burning bush that is not consumed.

Ex 3:3 - *Burning Bush*

³ AND MOSES SAID, I WILL NOW TURN ASIDE, AND SEE THIS GREAT SIGHT, **WHY THE BUSH IS NOT BURNT**. **KJV**

Saved By Death

Heb. 9:15 - *Mediator*

¹⁵ AND FOR THIS CAUSE **HE IS THE MEDIATOR OF THE NEW TESTAMENT,** THAT BY MEANS OF DEATH, FOR THE REDEMPTION OF THE TRANSGRESSIONS THAT WERE MADE . . . . **KJV**

That by means of death . . . .

There are three Greek words translated ***death***, brethren. This Greek word is ***thanatos***, which means either ***violent death***, or ***death which results from the separation of the personality*** (soul) ***from the Carnal Mind***.

It is hidden, brethren, so you have to pray about it, but ***the death that brings you into the New Covenant is the separation of your personality (soul) from your Carnal Mind.***

I declare to you with all the humility that I can muster, as I sit here half slain in the Spirit, that our Carnal Mind and our personality (soul) must separate and, more specifically, our personality (soul) must separate from the ***spirit*** of our Carnal Mind

Can you hear what I am saying? Let me read it to you again.

While you were under the Old Covenant, you were still in sin. Do you hear this?

That those who were sitting under the Old Covenant might receive the promise of an everlasting inheritance, by death.

The only way those of us who are under the Old Covenant, and still dying, will be experientially forgiven -- the only way that they will enter into **the New Covenant which is everlasting life** -- is by ***death***, and the Greek word ***death*** here, means the separation of the spirit of our Carnal Mind from our fallen personality (soul).

Jesus' death on the cross made Christ Jesus, the Everlasting Tabernacle, available to mortal humanity.

So, you see,

59

To enter into the Everlasting Tabernacle -- for our personality to join with the eternal life which is in Christ Jesus -- we must shed the spiritual blood of our Carnal Mind.

We enter into the Everlasting Tabernacle, which is Christ Jesus in the midst of us, by renouncing and destroying our fallen nature, which is our Carnal Mind, not by Jesus' death on the cross.

It was necessary for Jesus' physical body to die, so that Jesus, the whole man, could be resurrected in a higher spiritual form that can be grafted to fallen mankind.

Rom 6:22 – *Eternal Life*

> ²² BUT NOW BEING MADE FREE FROM SIN, AND BECOME SERVANTS TO GOD, YE HAVE YOUR FRUIT UNTO HOLINESS, AND THE END **EVERLASTING LIFE**. **KJV**

You see, when a man who is possessed of the Spirit of Christ dies, the Spirit of Christ within him rises and returns to the Father, and the personality (soul) that is joined to the Spirit of Christ rises with him. But the personality (soul) that is joined to the Carnal Mind, remains in the earth and dies

Eccl 3:21 – *Resurrection of The Soul*

> ²¹ **WHO KNOWETH THE SPIRIT OF MAN THAT GOETH UPWARD**, AND THE SPIRIT OF THE BEAST THAT GOETH DOWNWARD TO THE EARTH? **KJV**

When the personality of the man, Jesus, which was purified ***before He died***, separated from the Carnal Mind that was attached to the physical body that Jesus received, Jesus was able to defy the spiritual gravity that sought to hold Jesus' personality (soul) in the grave

Eph 4:8 – *Jesus Ascension*

> [8] WHEREFORE HE SAITH, **WHEN HE ASCENDED UP ON HIGH, HE LED CAPTIVITY CAPTIVE,** AND GAVE GIFTS UNTO MEN. **KJV**

We have read that we enter into the New Covenant only by death, *thanatos*, the death of our Carnal Mind.

We enter into the New Covenant by our death, brethren, but *NOT OUR PHYSICAL DEATH. OUR CARNAL MIND MUST DIE* for us to enter into the New Covenant.

The Lord has ordained that . . .

Our Carnal Mind shall die through the exposure of our sin nature, and that

Our personality (soul) shall be saved by being permanently joined to Christ Jesus who will fully purge her (our soul) from sin.

We have to do it His way!

QUESTIONS & ANSWERS

1.	*What happens to our physical body when we walk under the New Covenant with Christ?*

(A)	The purification of our personality gives us everlasting life right here in the flesh, and our bodies are preserved.

2.	*What does the resurrection of Christ mean?*

(A) The resurrection of Christ is the regeneration of the root of Adam of Creation who died in his sins.

3.	*Why is judgment in the flesh?*

(A)	So that we can learn to walk after the Spirit

1 Peter 4:6 – *Judged In The Flesh*

> [6] FOR, FOR THIS CAUSE WAS THE GOSPEL PREACHED ALSO TO THEM THAT ARE DEAD, THAT THEY **MIGHT BE JUDGED ACCORDING TO MEN IN THE FLESH, BUT LIVE ACCORDING TO GOD IN THE SPIRIT. KJV**

4.	*When will our mortal body (personality (soul)) be quickened (made alive)?*

(A) When Christ is raised from the dead in us

1 Cor 15:4 – *Christ Raised*

> [4] AND THAT HE WAS BURIED, AND THAT **HE ROSE AGAIN THE THIRD DAY** ACCORDING TO THE SCRIPTURES: **KJV**

(See, *The Christ*, LEM Message # 186 - Part 8).

5. *Does the quickening (coming to life) of our mortal body (personality (soul)) happen before or after our physical body is put in the grave?*

(A) Before. Our mortality (Carnal Mind) will be swallowed up into immortality (Christ Jesus)

2 Cor 5:4 – *Mortality Swallowed Up*

> [4] FOR WE THAT ARE IN THIS TABERNACLE DO GROAN, BEING BURDENED: NOT FOR THAT WE WOULD BE UNCLOTHED, BUT CLOTHED UPON, THAT **MORTALITY MIGHT BE SWALLOWED UP OF LIFE. KJV**

6. *Which Spirit raised Christ from the dead?*

(A) The Spirit of Christ

7. *Whose function is it to lead us to Christ?*

(A) The Holy Spirit.

8. *Name one purpose for receiving the Spirit of Christ.*

(A) So that He will graft Christ to our human spirit and form Christ Jesus in us

James 1:21 – *Engrafted Word*

> [21] WHEREFORE LAY APART ALL FILTHINESS AND SUPERFLUITY OF NAUGHTINESS, **AND RECEIVE WITH MEEKNESS THE ENGRAFTED WORD**, WHICH IS ABLE TO SAVE YOUR SOULS. **KJV**

9. *What is the ultimate result of Christ maturing in us?*

1 Cor 13:11 – *Spiritual Maturity*

[11] WHEN I WAS A CHILD, I SPAKE AS A CHILD, I UNDERSTOOD AS A CHILD, I THOUGHT AS A CHILD: BUT WHEN **I BECAME A MAN, I PUT AWAY CHILDISH THINGS. KJV**

Eph 4:13 – *The Stature of Christ*

[13] TILL WE ALL COME IN THE UNITY OF THE FAITH, AND OF THE KNOWLEDGE OF THE SON OF GOD, UNTO A PERFECT MAN, UNTO THE MEASURE OF **THE STATURE OF THE FULNESS OF CHRIST: KJV**

(A) Our personality (soul) will be preserved, and we will live forever.

10. *Did Paul say it was time to die?*

(A) No, he said it was time to be *offered up*

2 Tim 4:6 - *Paul Offered*

[6] FOR I AM NOW **READY TO BE OFFERED,** AND THE TIME OF MY DEPARTURE IS AT HAND. **KJV**

11. *What was Paul's job?*

(A) To bring forth the Doctrine of Christ.

12. *How do we know that we have not fully entered into the New Covenant yet?*

(A) We still get sick, age and die.

13.   *Are we saved by doctrine?*

(A) No. We are saved by union with the glorified Son of God and Christ Jesus, within us, the whole *New Man*

Eph 4:24 – *New Man*

> [24] AND THAT YE PUT ON **THE NEW MAN**, WHICH AFTER GOD IS CREATED IN RIGHTEOUSNESS AND TRUE HOLINESS. **KJV**

14.   *What is the first phase of the New Covenant?*

(A) *The forgiveness of sins* by faith, which permits us to enter into a relationship with the Father through a mediator. But we remain mortal.

15.   *What is the last phase of the New Covenant?*

(A) *Sinlessness*, which results in everlasting life

Mic 7:19 - *Sinless*

> [19] HE WILL TURN AGAIN, HE WILL HAVE COMPASSION UPON US; HE WILL SUBDUE OUR INIQUITIES; AND THOU WILT **CAST ALL THEIR SINS INTO THE DEPTHS OF THE SEA.** **KJV**

Heb 7:16 – *Eternal Life*

> [16] WHO IS MADE, NOT AFTER THE LAW OF A CARNAL COMMANDMENT, BUT AFTER **THE POWER OF AN ENDLESS LIFE.** **KJV**

16.   *Which two groups of people did the New Covenant go to?*

(A) To the Jew first, and then to the Gentiles

<u>Rom 1:16</u> – *To The Jew First*

¹⁶ FOR I AM NOT ASHAMED OF THE GOSPEL OF
CHRIST: FOR IT IS THE POWER OF GOD UNTO SALVATION TO
EVERY ONE THAT BELIEVETH; **TO THE JEW FIRST, AND ALSO
TO THE GREEK. KJV**

<u>Rom 2:10</u> – *To The Jew First*

¹⁰ BUT GLORY, HONOUR, AND PEACE, TO EVERY
MAN THAT WORKETH GOOD, **TO THE JEW FIRST, AND ALSO
TO THE GENTILE: KJV**

17. How did the Gentiles enter into God's Covenant?

(A) The Gospel went to the Gentiles when the Jews
stumbled

<u>Rom 11:15</u> – *Jews Cast Away*

¹⁵ FOR IF **THE CASTING AWAY OF THEM** BE THE
RECONCILING OF THE WORLD, WHAT SHALL THE RECEIVING
OF THEM BE, BUT LIFE FROM THE DEAD? **KJV**

18. What does it take to enter into the Sanctuary in the Heavenlies?

(A) Blood.

19. Whose blood do we enter in by?

(A) The spiritual blood of the Lord Jesus Christ makes
the Heavenly Sanctuary available to us . . .

<u>Heb 13:12</u> – *Sanctified By His Blood*

¹² WHEREFORE JESUS ALSO, **THAT HE MIGHT
SANCTIFY THE PEOPLE WITH HIS OWN BLOOD**, SUFFERED
WITHOUT THE GATE. **KJV**

Col 1:20 – *Peace Through His Blood*

> [20] AND, HAVING MADE PEACE **THROUGH THE BLOOD OF HIS CROSS**, BY HIM TO RECONCILE ALL THINGS UNTO HIMSELF; BY HIM, I SAY, WHETHER THEY BE THINGS IN EARTH, OR THINGS IN HEAVEN. **KJV**

. . . but we enter in by the shed blood of our Carnal Mind.

Heb 10:26 – *Sacrifice For Sins*

> [26] FOR IF WE SIN WILFULLY AFTER THAT WE HAVE RECEIVED THE KNOWLEDGE OF THE TRUTH, THERE REMAINETH NO MORE **SACRIFICE FOR SINS**, **KJV**

20.   What is our inheritance, and how can we enter in and appropriate it?

(A)   Christ Jesus, the heavenly sanctuary, is our inheritance. We enter in and begin to appropriate His spiritual life as our Carnal Mind dies.

21.   What do the animal sacrifices under the Levitical law of the Old Testament typify?

(A)   The bulls and goats that were sacrificed under the Levitical Law typify the human beastial nature called *the Carnal Mind.*

Rev 13:1 - *The Beast of The Unconscious Mind*

> [13] AND I STOOD UPON THE SAND OF THE SEA, **AND SAW A BEAST RISE UP OUT OF THE SEA**, HAVING SEVEN HEADS AND TEN HORNS, AND UPON HIS HORNS TEN CROWNS, AND UPON HIS HEADS THE NAME OF BLASPHEMY. **KJV**

It is our own Carnal Mind that must be sacrificed.

22. *Did Jesus enter in by his own blood?*

(A) The regenerated Adam within the man, Jesus of Nazareth, is the Heavenly Sanctuary. The personality of the man, Jesus, entered into that Heavenly Sanctuary within Himself by subjugating the Carnal Mind that that was attached to the physical body that he received when he was born into this world. . .

Col 1:20 – *The Blood of His Cross*

> [20] AND, HAVING MADE PEACE THROUGH THE BLOOD OF HIS CROSS, BY HIM TO RECONCILE ALL THINGS UNTO HIMSELF; BY HIM, I SAY, WHETHER THEY BE THINGS IN EARTH, OR THINGS IN HEAVEN. **KJV**

. . . and separating his human personality from it.

23. *Do the animal sacrifices of the Levitical Law typify the crucifixion of the Lord Jesus Christ?*

(A) No. They typify the sacrifice of the human beast, the Carnal Mind, also called *the Old Man*.

Rev 13:4 – *The Beast Worshipped*

> [4] AND THEY WORSHIPPED THE DRAGON WHICH GAVE POWER UNTO THE BEAST: **AND THEY WORSHIPPED THE BEAST**, SAYING, WHO IS LIKE UNTO THE BEAST? WHO IS ABLE TO MAKE WAR WITH HIM? **KJV**

Jesus sacrificed his resurrected life by which He could have lived in the earth in a human body, as an individual, immortal man, forever. But Jesus chose to be raised to an even higher form, glorification, by which His life is now being shared with all of humanity.

24. **What does the method of animal sacrifices of the Levitical Law typify?**

(A)   Roasting, the method of the Levitical sacrifices typifies the Lake of Fire, which is Christ Jesus in the individual.

The unconscious part of mortal man's Carnal Mind is typified by the *sea*, and the subconscious part of mortal man's Carnal Mind is the *beast*.

The sea evaporates when the Lake of Fire brings her waters to a boil, and the beast nature is roasted in the Lake of Fire and eaten by the glorified Jesus Christ, the High Priest.

25. **What form did the Lord Jesus Christ take after His resurrection?**

(A)   Jesus of Nazareth was blended into a glorified spiritual man, a form whereby his sinless life can be reproduced in mankind. The glorified Jesus became the source of the spiritual seed . . .

John 12:24 – *The Seed of Life*

> [24] VERILY, VERILY, I SAY UNTO YOU, **EXCEPT A CORN OF WHEAT FALL INTO THE GROUND** AND DIE, IT ABIDETH ALONE: BUT IF IT DIE, IT BRINGETH FORTH MUCH FRUIT. **KJV**

. . . that raises Christ in the individual from the dead. The glorified Jesus is saving fallen humanity from *hell* and *death* by giving us the seed of His resurrected life.

26. **What happens when the Lord Jesus Christ's sinless life is reproduced in a man?**

(A)   The sinless life of Christ Jesus sacrifices the Carnal Mind and presents the purified personality to the Father.

27.   *The sacrifices of the Levitical Law were consumed by the high priest. What does this typify?*

(A)   The Lord Jesus consumes the spiritual energy of Satan and Leviathan, the unconscious and subconscious parts of the Carnal Mind . . .

Heb 7:27 – *Satan Swallowed Up*

> [27] WHO NEEDETH NOT DAILY, AS THOSE HIGH PRIESTS, TO OFFER UP **SACRIFICE, FIRST FOR HIS OWN SINS, AND THEN FOR THE PEOPLE'S:** FOR THIS HE DID ONCE, WHEN HE OFFERED UP HIMSELF. **KJV**

. . . which typifies the reunification of the divided creation into one Blood under the authority of **the Lord Jesus Christ.**

28.   *When will we be raised from the dead?*

(A)   We are raised from the dead and enter into the life of the ages, which is the New Covenant, in three stages:

1. Our human spirit is resurrected (Redemption of the Spirit) when the Holy Spirit pierces it;

2. Our soul is resurrected (Salvation of the Soul) after it is joined to Christ Jesus, the Son of the Lord Jesus Christ in a man; and

3. Our physical body is transformed (Glorification of the whole man) into a spiritual body after it is spiritually melted, and then blended with the New, Inner Man.

1 Cor 6:17 – *Life Is Union With God*

> [17] BUT **HE THAT IS JOINED UNTO THE LORD IS ONE SPIRIT. KJV**

The Old Man

Satan is the unconscious part of the Carnal Mind, the mind of mortal man,

Leviathan is the subconscious part of the Carnal Mind, the mind of mortal man, and

Cain is the conscious part of the Carnal Mind, the mind of mortal man.

The Devil is the personality (soul) that is in agreement with the Carnal Mind.

The Devil is the Old Man who is passing away.

The New Man

The Lord Jesus Christ is the unconscious part of the Christ Mind,

Christ Jesus is the subconscious part of the Christ Mind,

Christ is the male seed of Jesus Christ grafted to Abel and the conscious part of the Christ mind.

Abel is the root of spiritual intelligence in Adam of Creation who died in his sins. Christ is grafted to Abel.

The New Man is the personality (soul) that is in agreement with the Mind of Christ.

Christ Jesus is the New Man who is being born in mankind.

Christ Jesus is the only Mediator between God and mankind.

<u>1 Tim 2:5</u> – *Union That Produces Life*

⁵ FOR THERE IS ONE GOD, AND **ONE MEDIATOR** BETWEEN GOD AND MEN, THE MAN CHRIST JESUS; **KJV**

TABLE OF REFERENCES

RECOMMENDED, ADDITIONAL STUDY:

LEM MESSAGE #186 – 12 Parts

CHRIST

ABOUT THE AUTHOR

Sheila R. Vitale is the Spiritual Leader, Founding Teacher, and Pastor of *Living Epistles Ministries (LEM)*. She moves in the offices of Teacher of Apostolic Doctrine, Prophet, Evangelist and Pastor, has an international following, and has been expounding on the Scripture through a unique spiritual lens for nearly three decades.

She has written more than 50 books based on the Old and New Testaments including *Ephraim, Man of the Earth* and *The Eagle Ascended (OT)*, and *Salvation* and *Not Without Blood (NT)*. She has also rendered original spiritual interpretations of Biblical texts such as *The Woman in The Well (John, Chapter 4)* and *First Corinthians, Chapter 11*. Her unique, Multi-Part Message style is seen in *LEM* Serial Messages such as *A Place Teeming With Life* (9 Parts) and *Quantum Mechanics in Creation* (18 Parts). Each Part of a Multi-Part Message Series can also be enjoyed as a complete and independent study. In addition, she has defined, explained, illustrated and demonstrated hundreds of spiritual principles throughout more than 1,000 *LEM* Lectures.

Her signature work, however, is the three volumes of *The Alternate Translation Bible (ATB)*: *The Alternate Translation of The Old Testament*, *The Alternate Translation of The New Testament* and *The Alternate Translation of the Book of Revelation*. *The Alternate Translation Bible* is a work in progress (*The ATB Project*). Accordingly, additional spiritual interpretations of both whole and partial Chapters are added from time to time, as they are rendered. The most up-to-date versions of *The ATB Project* may be found online at *The LEM Website* (*LivingEpistles.org*). *The ATB* is a *spiritual interpretation* of the Scripture and is not intended to replace traditional translations.

She also analyzed the Greek text of *The Book of Revelation* and preached extensively on it in the early years of *The ATB Project*. During that time she produced 197 distinct *Message Parts*, under 29 specific *Message Titles*, all of which deal with *The Book of Revelation*. Also, many of her books such as, *Adam and The Two Judgments* and *A Study in Unconscious Mind Control*, have been translated into Spanish, as well as *The Book of Revelation*.

Pastor Vitale is an illustrator of spiritual principles, a researcher, a translator and a reviewer of the Modern Social Trends of Family and Culture, as they are revealed through TV programs *(The Sopranos),* movies *(The Matrix* and *The Edge of Tomorrow)* and plays *(Wicked)*. She also writes for the *LEM Blog*.

She travels domestically, as well as internationally, preaching and teaching Judeo-Christian Spiritual Philosophy, and has donated Audio Libraries of her Lectures to other ministries in Africa, Asia, Europe and North America,

Pastor Vitale serves *LEM* in a range of spiritual, educational, and administrative functions from *The Selden Centre, LEM* headquarters in Selden, New York. She is also a philanthropic individual who supports the *Lighthouse Mission (Patchogue, NY) and HGM – Mission of Hope – Haiti, and other* charitable organizations. She also supports community services such as the *Terryville Fire Department*.

In her spare time, Pastor Vitale enjoys watching movies, attending plays and partaking of cuisines from different cultures. An avid traveler, she has visited several countries in Europe and Africa as well as many cities in the United States.

BEGINNINGS, INSPIRATION AND CALLING

Pastor Vitale began her spiritual journey as a child when her Jewish mother enrolled her in the Hebrew school of an Orthodox synagogue. She experienced the Spirit of God for the first time there in such a profound way that she wept. But after that, when she was only eleven years old, she became very ill and was taken to Mount Sinai Hospital in New York City. She almost died there and has battled with life-threatening health issues ever since. Nevertheless, a deep longing for God continued to pursue her until several years later when she desperately wanted to attend Yeshiva (Jewish high school), but could not. Her secular parents approved of her choice, but could not afford the tuition.

Much later, after years of searching, she once again experienced the Spirit that had brought her to tears in the synagogue of her youth, but this time it was at *Gospel Revivals Ministries*, a Pentecostal church where Deliverance Ministry was emphasized. She had a desire to understand the Bible since she was a child, but Scripture was difficult for her and she struggled with the text. Nevertheless, she read one Chapter of the Bible every day until, one day, *her spiritual eyes opened* and she saw an angel holding a little book.

After that, she attended as many as five teaching services each week for about seven years, the latter part of which she edited *Pastor Holzhauser's* books. But several more years had to pass before *the eyes of her understanding opened even further* and she began to receive *Revelation Knowledge of the Scripture.* She understood at that time that the angel she had seen was the angel of Revelation 10:8.

After about seven years of learning *Deliverance Ministry* and *The Doctrine of Sonship (Bill Britton)* from *Pastor Holzhauser,* she studied the Bible independently under the influence and direction of the Holy Spirit.

In **1998** she began teaching Apostolic Doctrine.

In **1990** she spent three months in Stony Brook Hospital where she recovered from an incurable disease, defeating premature death, once again, and went on to resume teaching and managing *LEM.*

In **1992** she journeyed to Africa for the first time, where she was called to the office of Evangelist.

In the **mid-1990s,** she began to Pastor in addition to being a Teacher of Apostolic Doctrine, a Prophet and an Evangelist, thus, satisfying all five offices of *The Ministry of the Lord Jesus Christ to His Church.*

LIVING EPISTLES MINISTRIES

Pastor Vitale was happy fellowshipping at *Gospel Revivals Ministries* but, eventually, she desired a deeper and more spiritual understanding of the Word of God. One day, after crying out to Jesus about her need, she was amazed to hear Him ask her if she would teach. Her initial response was that she did not see how it would be possible since she was already working a full-time job, despite her poor health. But after the Lord asked her for a second and then a third time, she reluctantly agreed, believing that He would empower her to do the job. Shortly thereafter, in the latter part of 1987, she began to teach her own brand of Judeo-Christian Spiritual Philosophy.

The Lord Jesus Christ named the work *Living Epistles Ministries* in 1988.

The first *LEM* meetings were casual and spontaneous gatherings of friends and fellow deliverance workers in Pastor Vitale's home. After that, they were held in the business office of one of the brethren. Pastor Vitale delivered her first formal message entitled *The Truth About Witchcraft in January of 1988*, followed by *The Seduction of Eve* in April of the same year. After that, she prepared and taught weekly messages including *Signs of Apostleship* and *Lazarus & The Rich Man.* The meetings eventually increased to two and then three each week.

Sometime after that, she learned that the Lord Jesus Christ was revealing spiritual principles from the Hebrew text of the Old Testament through her teachings, and she used those spiritual principles to begin to unlock the mysteries of the New Testament, as well. Today she understands that the Scripture is a spiritual document that must be spiritually discerned if it is to be understood correctly, and calls that spiritual understanding ***The Doctrine of Christ***.

    LEM publishes a wide range of material, including books, e-books, spiritual interpretations of the Scripture and transcripts of many of Pastor Vitale's Lectures and on-line meetings, all of which, as well as the entire *Alternate Translation Bible,* may be viewed free of charge on the *LEM* website (*LivingEpistles.org*). She also has an *Author's Website* where all of her books, as well as several photographs of herself and a short biography are displayed (Amazon.com/author/SheilaVitale). Paperback and digital versions of *LEM* books may be purchased through *Amazon, Google Books* and *Barnes & Noble*.

    LEM provides free video livestreams through YouTube and other Internet Platforms . . .

    @LivingEpistlesMinistries (2016 – Sept. 2022)
    @LivingEpistlesMinistriesLEM ((Oct. 2022 – Ongoing)
    @LivingEpistlesMinistries (LEM disciples)

    . . . as well as two channels of ***Shortclips*** where short, focused messages of about 15 minutes each are posted:

    @shortclipsbysheilar.vitale3334 (2016 – Sept. 2022)
    @ShortClips-SheilaVitale (Oct. 2022 – Ongoing)

    LEM donates a significant percentage of its income to other Christian ministries and organizations that advocate for Christian values and defend the United States Constitution.

PASTOR VITALE TODAY

    Today Pastor Vitale continues to dedicate her life to teaching the spiritual principles of the Bible and focuses daily on studying, writing and preaching powerful messages from *The Selden Centre,* LEM/CCK's headquarters at Selden, New York.

SALVATION

An In-Depth Study

Sheila R. Vitale
Living Epistles Ministries

THE TRUTH

ABOUT BAPTISM

A Study in Baptism & Tongues

Sheila R. Vitale
Living Epistles Ministries

PHASES OF CREATION

Sheila R. Vitale

Living Epistles Ministries

Living Epistles Ministries
Sheila R. Vitale
Pastor, Teacher & Founder
Judeo-Christian Spiritual Philosophy
PO Box 562, Port Jefferson Station, New York 11776, USA
LivingEpistles.org
or
Books@LivingEpistles.org